Orange

Evaluating the ROI from Learning

Bury College

How ~ ~~~~~~~~ ~ ~ased Trai~~~g

Paul Kearns is Director of PWL, an HR and training evaluation and measurement consultancy. He has worked in the field of HR, training, development and learning since 1978 and began specialising in training evaluation and ROI in 1991. He has a global reputation as a consultant, facilitator, trainer and conference speaker. Paul can be contacted at PWL on +44 (0)117 9146984 or email paulkearns@blueyonder.co.uk

*Trying to get people to learn without evaluation
is like trying to make wine without grapes.*

The Chartered Institute of Personnel and Development is the leading publisher of books and reports for personnel and training professionals, students, and all those concerned with the effective management and development of people at work. For details of all our titles, please contact the publishing department:

tel: 020 8612 6200

e-mail publish@cipd.co.uk

The catalogue of all CIPD titles can be viewed on the CIPD website:

www.cipd.co.uk/bookstore

Evaluating the ROI from Learning

How to Develop Value-based Training

Paul Kearns

Chartered Institute of Personnel and Development

Published by the Chartered Institute of Personnel and Development,
151 The Broadway, London SW19 1JQ

First published 2005

Reprinted 2006, 2007

Design by Fakenham Photosetting, Fakenham, Norfolk

Typeset by Fakenham Photosetting, Fakenham, Norfolk

Printed in Great Britain by The Cromwell Press, Trowbridge, Wiltshire

British Library Cataloguing in Publication Data

A catalogue of this manual is available from the British Library

ISBN 1-84398-078-9
ISBN-13 978-1-84398-078-0

The views expressed in this manual are the author's own and may not necessarily reflect those
of the CIPD.

The CIPD has made every effort to trace and acknowledge copyright holders. If any source has
been overlooked, CIPD Enterprises would be pleased to redress this for future editions.

Chartered Institute of Personnel and Development

151 The Broadway, London SW19 1JQ

Tel: 020 8612 6200

Email: cipd@cipd.co.uk   Website: www.cipd.co.uk

Incorporated by Royal Charter   Registered Charity No. 1079797

■ CONTENTS

■ LISTS OF FIGURES

■ INTRODUCTION

The way we evaluate the effectiveness of our training interventions simply has to improve. To give you just one example: the CIPD Training and Development Survey 2004 showed that 77 per cent of respondents were increasing their use of coaching but that, while 75 per cent of respondents used feedback from the coachee to evaluate the coaching programme, only 37 per cent assessed coaching programmes against their original objectives and only 29 per cent evaluated any business performance indicators.

What is the point in making any business investment – for that is what training is – if you don't establish whether it has achieved its goals or delivered any improvement in performance? Would you spend years investing money in a company pension plan without evaluating its performance or assessing whether it was going to be able to meet its objective of providing you with a comfortable retirement? A bad example perhaps, but you see what I mean.

Whether we are considering supporting an employee in their MBA studies, offering them the facility of a corporate university, providing e-learning, classroom training or coaching should we not be following a sound set of principles that underpin effective learning? That is assuming of course that by 'effective' learning we mean learning that simultaneously ensures that both the individual and the organisation perform better. To be even more precise, let us assume that 'performance' means that the individual's efforts ultimately add value in the same way that any other investment may add value. Effective learning reduces costs, in public sector organisations it improves service levels, in private sector businesses it increases revenue or improves the share price.

Like all investments, provision of training involves decision-making. If you want the choices you make to add value to your organisation, rather than simply consuming it, then you must understand how to evaluate the return on your investment in learning. The point of this book is to show you that effective evaluation isn't just about justifying your job, it's about making value-based choices that will improve the impact of the training you provide.

SO WHAT CAN YOU EXPECT FROM AN EVALUATION SYSTEM?

This book might not be able to resolve all your initial questions, preconceived ideas and possible misconceptions about evaluation, but I would just ask you to consider the following statements. They are meant to provide an instantaneous flavour of what you will encounter throughout this book and should serve to manage your expectations:

- Evaluation is a simple subject if you keep it simple.

- Evaluation is a means to an end – that is individual and organisational performance – it should never be seen as an end in itself.

- You will need an evaluation system and some tools and techniques, as well as an evaluation model, if you are going to get the most out of evaluation.

- Don't come to evaluation from a defensive standpoint. It should not be used to justify your existence as a trainer – so always think positively.

- Don't always expect to hear only good news, negative feedback in evaluation is equally important.

- Evaluation is about learning from our mistakes just as much as it is about celebrating our successes.

- If you and the training team are the only ones evaluating you are probably doing it wrong.

- If you are producing lots of paperwork and data you are probably doing it wrong.

- The single, most important lesson to learn in evaluation is **do it before you do the training.**

- Evaluation should be part of the training design.

- Every learning intervention should be considered on its own merits, from an evaluation perspective. There is no such thing as a standard, generic learning solution.

- There is a big difference in practice between 'evalua<u>tion</u>' – the concept and theory – and 'evalua<u>ting</u>' – the activity of actually trying to measure something.

- If you understand the theory and practice of evalua<u>tion</u> you will not have to do too much evalua<u>ting.</u>

- Happy sheets are <u>not</u> evaluation.
- Knowledge and skills tests are <u>not</u> evaluation.
- The only true measure for evaluation is always value.

Now most of these points are very simple to grasp but it is also very important to understand fully the theory that underpins them.

SOUND THEORY IS CRUCIAL TO EFFECTIVE PRACTICE

Training practitioners have a tendency to keep the theory of training separate from its practice: a point that will be made abundantly clear in Chapter 2. However, you cannot be a totally effective, professional trainer without having a solid grounding in theory. Furthermore, the theory should inform every aspect of the practical application of evaluation. Those who fully understand the theory are much more likely to avoid all the problems and pitfalls often associated with evaluation. Being totally at ease with the theory will give you much more confidence in the practical application of evaluation. It will help you to explain to others exactly what you are doing and why you are doing it; including inquisitive or reluctant managers and employees. Moreover, the theory presented here can be applied anywhere, in any organisational context.

One immediate reaction you may have when reading the theory is that you do not like it. Evaluation is measurement and measuring what we do makes us more accountable. It puts us under greater pressure to achieve. Measurement is also about being specific and clear about our objectives. You may not feel comfortable being that specific about what someone is meant to learn and how they should apply that learning. Whatever your personal views, however, it should be pointed out that I did not invent the rules on evaluation. Please do not shoot the messenger!

In fact nothing in this book represents an invention. The theories, diagrams and models merely explain what evaluation is and how to use it. They are meant to be simple, yet not simplistic. When you read about the 3 Box System in Chapter 6, for example, you should be able to apply it to your own training efforts immediately.

Evaluation is, and always should have been, an integral part of the training cycle (see Chapter 2). What I have attempted to do is put it in its complete and rightful context by showing how this theory connects with Kolb's learning cycle, the Plan Do Check Act (PDCA) cycle, Investors in People, the philosophy and theories of continuous improvement, organisational development and knowledge management. When all of these connections are made you should be able to see what a crucial and powerful part evaluation will play in learning.

The various elements that form the evaluation methodology here could be regarded as 'the rules of the game'. The only reason trainers have had so many problems with evaluation, for so many years, is the fact that, either they do not understand these rules or, even if they do, they try to play the learning game with a different set of rules. People who constantly infringe the rules, though, normally end up having to leave the field.

One of the best illustrations of this occurred recently (February 2004) when I met a training manager on one of my workshops who I remembered from a meeting some years ago. When we previously met he worked in the financial services industry and told me he was not too concerned with evaluation because he had won several awards for his training. I noticed, though, that he was now working for a different company and asked why he had moved. He replied that at his previous employer a new CEO came on board when the business was not doing so well and he was only impressed by results, not awards. Consequently the training manager, along with the rest of his award-winning team, was made redundant. That is why he finally decided to come on the evaluation workshop.

WHO SAYS EVALUATION IS A DIFFICULT SUBJECT?

One thing this book is not going to do, however, is provide a critique of all the other evaluation models available. If any existing models had worked particularly well we would not still be discussing the subject. In fact only one model will warrant any serious mention: the Kirkpatrick Model (see Chapter 3). This will be used to provide some of the basic building blocks for the ultimate in evaluation methodologies: the Baseline Model (Chapter 4). This might appear a rather arrogant stance on my part, but for the fact that I make no claims to have invented this model, any more than Halley invented 'his' comet.

Unfortunately, though, some academics and quite a few consultants make a good living out of the evaluation debate and plenty of confusion still surrounds the subject. Some training providers also like to cloud the issue to protect their 'products', whose efficacy (or lack of it) might be exposed by true evaluation. That is one of the barriers that will have to be overcome. Effective evaluation sorts the wheat from the chaff remarkably easily and quickly. It will also expose any charlatans; but don't expect them to go willingly into the night.

It is to the great shame of the training 'profession' that it has failed to produce a universally accepted and workable evaluation methodology. This has allowed the profession to be infiltrated by anyone who wants to put the title 'trainer' or 'developer' on their business card. Without a commonly agreed standard for measuring training effectiveness they are immune to challenge on grounds of their lack of any 'professional' credentials or evidence that their methods work. Surely, anyone who takes their work and their professionalism seriously will not regard this as a satisfactory state of affairs for one minute.

ONCE YOU HAVE CRACKED THE EVALUATION CODE YOU CAN CONCENTRATE ON LEARNING

It is ironic that so many training teams have spent so much time and energy on evaluation when there is no recognised way to do it effectively. They have persisted though, because they believe that, somehow, producing figures to reveal the benefits of training is the reason we should carry out evaluation. In the worst cases, where training departments are under pressure to justify their existence, mountains of evaluation data and reports are produced. Such efforts completely miss the point.

Evaluation is only a step in the journey towards the ultimate destination of organisational value. The journey itself is learning – individual and organisational. It is also a never-ending journey, so any evaluation is just a stop along the way.

Having just read the above paragraph you might still not see where evaluation fits into the total picture or how important it is. As we will see later, the difference that evaluation makes to the whole learning process is immense. The best learning organisation in the world, Toyota, has a market value ($110 billion in November 2003) greater than Ford, GM and Daimler Chrysler put together. They make very reliable cars, much more efficiently than anyone else. They have only been able to attain this pre-eminent position by constantly learning how to improve. If they continue to improve in this way (which I am absolutely confident they will) then at some stage in the future the other automotive producers mentioned will not exist as we currently know them, if at all.

That, on its own, should begin to indicate why it is worth getting this subject of evaluation right once and for all. Imagine if every hospital, police force, public sector body and government department, as well as every commercial organisation, managed to learn how to improve to this same extent? Just think what a difference this would make to society as a whole. Evaluation is not just a subject for the training team: it is the source of enormous wealth creation, especially for those organisations, like Toyota, that understand it and learn how to use it before everyone else does. It is the subject of learning that we should be promoting here, not evaluation, but you cannot have one without the other. Evaluation is a means to a very important end.

Many trainers reading this will immediately retort that they are already helping people to learn. In fact many trainers would now much prefer to call themselves learning specialists. They talk about 'learning to learn' and many organisations have policies where any learning is assumed to be a good idea. Unfortunately though, their relative performance is constantly deteriorating. Learning for the sake of it is of no use if your main competitor is always learning to improve.

Of course, we would all agree that it is a good thing that people want to learn and most of us would support the notion of 'lifelong learning' even if none of us could define exactly what it means. How else would society make progress without learning? We all learn something new every day just by reading a newspaper, watching the TV or even conversing with friends and colleagues. If anyone could be bothered to measure everything we learn the volume of new knowledge that we manage to assimilate would probably stagger us. But not all learning is necessarily good and, from an organisational perspective, learning only brings benefits if it is effectively applied in the workplace.

So this book is really about using evaluation to gauge the benefits of training and development *in organisations*. This is a very different proposition to looking at learning per se. As soon as an organisation decides to devote resources to training and development activity it is making a choice. There is an opportunity cost; would it be better to spend the money on something else? It therefore needs to have a method for prioritising where it allocates its resources ('why don't we spend that money on marketing instead?'). Moreover, it should definitely want to establish whether its investment was a wise one. It can only do any of this if it has a robust evaluation methodology.

Despite all these obvious reasons for measuring the benefits of training, every organisation I know has been prepared to spend vast amounts of money on training without having any of these critical elements in place. They tend to take the view, as they do with spending on advertising, that while they know half of the money is wasted they cannot do anything about it because they do not know which half. That cynical attitude is no longer tenable when a proper evaluation system is available. With evaluation (and especially the 3 Box System in Chapter 6) not only will they find out which half of their training budget is wasted, they will also know exactly what to do about it.

So let us get this subject of evaluation sorted out once and for all and then we can all get on with the really interesting and satisfying job of helping our organisations, and the people who work in them, to learn as much as possible with as great a benefit as possible.

SO WHAT'S IN IT FOR YOU?

Already this might be starting to look like a challenge, so what is in it for you? Perhaps the most obvious benefit is likely to be a higher salary. After I spoke at the first UKHRD conference in May 2004 a delegate, who told me he had already heard about my approach to evaluation at an earlier event, said he was convinced that it had given him the edge at the final interview for his new job, which had increased his salary by £5,000. This was obviously very pleasing to hear but, compared to many other professions, training and development has not been particularly well paid (an extra £5,000 would be small reward for a lawyer). This is probably for two main reasons. First, there is no barrier to entry for those who have not obtained a professional qualification (unlike lawyers or accountants). Second, jobs that appear to have a direct and significant impact on the bottom line tend to attract greater rewards. Training does not currently satisfy either of these particular criteria very well.

This book is not intending to do much about the first of these problems, except indirectly. Effective trainers have nothing to fear from evaluation. Evaluation will raise the credibility and professionalism of the training world enormously. Those who can demonstrate results will attract the rewards they deserve. Those who cannot will, hopefully, be consigned to history along with all the other snake oil salesmen of yesteryear.

If the start and the end of any learning process are focused on creating a significant business impact, then trainers will be seen as directly contributing to organisational performance. When we come to the subject of ROI in Chapter 5 this will be translated into real £s and percentage returns in the same way as any other business appraisal decision. Consequently, trainers will at last attain the status of true business partners on a par with any other managerial profession.

As the subject of evaluation unfolds you will also see many other personal benefits, with an increase in job satisfaction and the development of a much wider and more influential role. However, evaluation is certainly not the preserve of the training department. Unless everyone else in the organisation is supporting the introduction of evaluation it is not going to happen.

SO WHAT'S IN IT FOR EVERYONE ELSE?

Many managers have a blind spot when it comes to training and development. They cannot see the real value in it. However supportive they are, training will always come second best to running their department or delivering their immediate business objectives. Of course, operational managers will always have day-to-day problems that flare up now and again and require immediate action (eg a serious customer complaint). How often, though, do they undertake a proper root cause analysis to find out why it flared up in the first place? If they did, how often would they be able to identify the training and development needs that generate such problems (eg a member of staff failing to fully explain an important contractual clause)? When we come to the subject of single-and double-loop learning in Chapter 6 we will see that evaluation sits right at the heart of a manager's drive to develop their people fully and properly. So what is the motivation for managers to play their part?

Very simply, they need to see evaluation as something that will make their lives easier. If they perceive it as a chore or an extra burden they will not afford it the time and effort required. Initially you will have to 'sell' them the idea of evaluation by showing some quick wins, some instant results. They will probably also need to take most of the credit in order to reinforce their new behaviour. This will be very much part of the overall equation, they will only own the process themselves if they feel it is beneficial to them.

Then, of course, we have to consider the individual employee or 'trainee' themselves. If we are going to evaluate their training it will make them more accountable for it. If they want the organisation to invest some money in their development their part of the bargain will be to show some improvement as a result. That might be a very fresh perspective for most employees who are used to viewing training as an optional employment benefit or even a good way to meet colleagues for a few days a year, out of the office and away from work.

The 'sales pitch' to employees has to be that evaluation will make their own personal development more rewarding. Really effective personal development is the sort of thing they will want to show on their cv, not just attendance on a generic training course. Effective development will play a key part in their ability to market themselves to other employers should they ever need or want to.

In short, the solution to the evaluation question does not rest entirely in the hands of the trainers. It has to be the responsibility of everyone involved in the learning process: senior management, line managers and employees themselves. Evaluation will make a trainer's life easier and much more fulfilling. It will do the same for all other stakeholders when the trainer explains what is involved. This will become much clearer as we move on to explore the whole subject of evaluation in greater detail.

1 ■ BUILDING THE FOUNDATIONS FOR EVALUATION

1 ■ HOW TO MAKE MANAGERS UNDERSTAND YOUR ROLE

This chapter may seem like a digression from our main purpose of describing a route through the evaluation maze but, as we shall soon see, this maze is overgrown with ignorance and negative managerial attitudes to training, development and learning. Trimming this back and replanting some new ideas is critical to making any progress in evaluation. Knowing and fully understanding the Baseline Model (see Chapter 4) is a prerequisite, but the context in which it is used is even more important.

The context that all trainers face is one of managers who want us to react immediately to their apparent training needs but who will not allow us the time to do a proper and thorough needs analysis. Yet we react to their demands at our peril and to the detriment of both the trainees and, ironically, the managers themselves.

■ REACTING TO 'TRAINING NEEDS' OR HOW TO SAY 'NO'

Many years ago, when I had only been in my new job as head of training for a couple of weeks, our technical director came into my office and asked me if I could organise some presentation skills training for his team of engineers. I have to admit that I did not particularly like the way he just *expected* me to deal with his requests immediately, without any prior discussion. So my first reaction was 'Can we sit down and talk about exactly what you want?' This was not the reaction he had been used to from my predecessor. He seemed very impatient and more or less intimated 'What is there to talk about?' As far as he was concerned it was a simple matter of sending his engineers on a course.

I advised him that there was a great deal more to training than just sending people on courses but he just tried to pull rank on me and replied that, as a director, he was entitled to ask for, and get, what he wanted when he wanted it. I told him this might have been the sort of relationship he had with my predecessor but that was not the way I worked (and I had equal management team status). With a huff he said he had more important matters to deal with, turned on his heels and strode out of my office.

At the time of this event (1988) I had 10 years' experience under my belt but I was working quite intuitively. I was still developing my own approach to training and development but I had already started asking myself some tough questions about what made the difference between effective and ineffective training. One clear conclusion I had reached, however, was that trainers should never be bullied into doing something with which they did not agree. Any manager/trainer relationship based on the master/servant model is unlikely to be that fruitful. So I made sure this director had cause to re-think some of his own preconceived ideas and prejudices about training.

A few weeks later, when he and the rest of the management team had started to get used to the idea of a training function 'with attitude', he raised the subject of presentation skills once more. I said the only way to move forward was to ask him more questions about exactly what he needed. This time he reluctantly agreed.

The first question I asked him was why his engineers needed presentation skills. He replied that they were required to make presentations at tender meetings with prospective customers. I then asked whether any of them had already made presentations. He said only one of them had so far, as the engineering manager previously undertook this job. 'How did the first engineer's presentation go?', I enquired. 'Terribly.' Why? 'He was hopeless – and the MD was there to witness it. He thinks it may have cost us the contract.' Now the reason for the sudden training need was abundantly clear. It is amazing how often training is the first knee-jerk reaction to an underlying problem.

I then asked a whole series of questions about whether this engineer had any natural aptitude for presenting, how he was chosen, how much notice he had been given, how much he had prepared. The reply was that he was 'thrown in at the eleventh hour because the engineering manager was not available.' Obviously the damage had already been done, so the next questions focused on how many presentations were expected to happen during the rest of the year and whether all engineers would have to make them. The director did not know. I told him that if he did not know the answer to this question then he had not yet established a clear training need.

The lessons from this anecdote are clear. Reacting to ill-defined 'training needs' is no way to run a training function. However, part of the solution to this problem is to educate operational managers to adopt a much more mature and intelligent attitude to training and development.

It would be very easy for me to be judgmental about the way managers, at all levels, view training and development. I have had some horrendous personal experiences over the years, with managers removing staff from courses, openly denigrating the training function and doing their best to subvert any efforts to offer their staff any effective development. However, I had to admit to myself, many years ago, that such 'bad' attitudes were at least as much to do with me as them. If managers did not support development it was probably because they had previously worked with training teams who demanded much of their time and offered no results in return. Or maybe no one had explained to them that development was intended to make their managerial lives easier and not be a chore. Certainly, they had never seen the real value of training, in ROI terms, with their own eyes.

There is no point in being judgmental on this point. You have to work with whoever you have to work with. You can only start from where you are. You have to find out what a senior manager's perception of training is before you can convince them of its value. So ask your CEO, or one of the operational directors, which of the following statements most closely matches their current perception of the value of training.

These are obviously loaded statements and any intelligent manager will realise that. Do they see training as a necessary evil, an overhead they have come to accept begrudgingly? Or are they committed to training? If they are committed how do they demonstrate that? Does putting more money into the training budget signal real commitment to learning?

THE DIFFERING PERCEPTIONS OF THE VALUE OF TRAINING

- 'I regard training as an overhead because it is something I know we have to do. Like all overheads though, I want to keep it to a minimum.'

- 'I'm very committed to training because I believe it is beneficial. I think it is right, therefore, to always allocate a percentage of paybill to it.'

- 'I regard training as an investment. I know we have to do some basic training but I also think training can improve the way we perform. However, we should treat it like any other investment and always ensure that we use such resources wisely.'

They will see quite clearly that the first perception is meant to be from a manager who is reluctant to see any potential for added value from training and are unlikely to choose this one, even if it most accurately reflects their own views.

The second statement is probably closer to most managers' perceptions. They have an inner belief system that tells them training is a good idea but they will not have put much more thought into it than that. Fixing the training budget in advance and linking it to paybill is their simplistic way of satisfying this inner need whilst not having to worry further about the subject.

The third statement is obviously the most enlightened of the three and any manager who wants to appear to be saying the right things will choose this one. This is, after all, not only the most intelligent answer but also the most mature. Training should always have been a wise investment and perceived as such, so it should not simply have funds thrown at it. This also implies, therefore, that each training investment should be judged on its own merits. There is no suggestion here that the simplistic formula of a percentage of paybill will do.

Of course, we could compose many more statements to reveal the distinctions and even nuances between different perceptions of the value of training, but these cover the three main categories. Surely, the perception we would like directors and managers to have is that training is just like any other investment and we should be deploying resources wisely, not as an act of faith or as part of some public relations exercise. The aim is to ensure all stakeholders eventually choose the third statement, so we will now look at how the Learning Maturity Scale will help you to achieve this.

THE LEARNING MATURITY SCALE

The development of the Learning Maturity Scale (see Figure 1.1) grew from a need to help training and development teams gauge where their own organisation is in terms of its attitude to learning. It is a scale that asks whether your organisation is getting as much value out of learning as it could. It also asks how intelligently and maturely the board, managers, all other employees and the training team themselves, approach the whole subject of learning. In fact, this scale really provides an objective framework against which all stakeholders can articulate how they see the training function and the role they expect from it.

This scale reflects a combination of my own professional experiences over the last 25 years and a view of what the future might hold. So it has a historical, as well as a future, perspective. It is intended to show the evolution of how organisations train and learn. It is also a cumulative scale, every organisation needing a training administration function (stage 1) which forms an essential building block for subsequent stages.

Most important of all though, it is intended to encapsulate the views of everyone in the organisation. Apart from the perspective of managers and trainers, what about

Figure 1.1   Where are you on the Learning Maturity Scale?

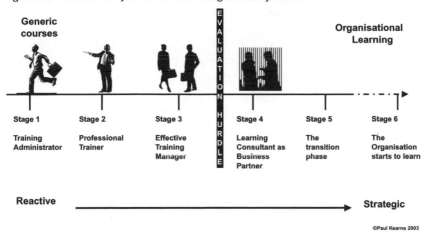

Generic courses			E V A L U A T I O N	Organisational Learning		

Stage 1	Stage 2	Stage 3	H U R D L E	Stage 4	Stage 5	Stage 6
Training Administrator	Professional Trainer	Effective Training Manager		Learning Consultant as Business Partner	The transition phase	The Organisation starts to learn

Reactive ———————————————————————————▶ Strategic

©Paul Kearns 2003

individual employees? Do they believe that their own development is inter-linked with the way the organisation performs? Would they take offence if the organisation chose not to support their own training if there was no anticipated organisational benefit? Do they just see training as another item on their cv to impress a future employer?

It is a relatively simple graphic, which attempts to convey a whole range of concepts, attitudes and practices. The intention is to gauge where the organisation is at a point in time and to shift its maturity level to the right. This shift from left to right also marks a shift from 'reactive' training mode to a 'strategic' approach to learning; where learning itself is a source of competitive advantage. So let us explore each of the stages on the scale in turn in order to build up a picture that is both multi-dimensional and dynamic.

THE SIX STAGES OF THE MATURITY SCALE

Stage 1. Training administration only

Although administration is a basic building block of any training function, if its only function is to book courses for employees this represents the most immature view of training that an organisation can hold. Stage 1 organisations still exist though. The CEO and board do not really have any interest in training and they would not even begin to understand the distinction between training and learning. All they are interested in is ensuring training (or lack of it) does not give rise to any problems (ie compliance, regulatory requirements, health and safety). Such organisations want to spend the absolute minimum amount on training. They will usually allocate a percentage of wage bill to the training budget each year, or even just a fixed monetary amount, without any assessment of real training needs.

Organisations at stage 1 just run a menu of generic courses (eg standard supervisors' modules). Occasionally, certain managers ask for other, one-off programmes (usually as a knee-jerk response to a specific problem that has just arisen, such as a serious accident or a tribunal hearing) and the funds are then allocated accordingly. So training is either unfocused, merely reactive or both. The only training measures in place at stage 1 are the numbers of people attending courses (training days) and the main concern is minimising the average cost per head. This is because training is perceived as an overhead rather than as an investment.

Of course, training administrators provide an important role in ensuring joining instructions are sent out promptly and efficiently but they add little value if the training needs analysis (TNA) process is poor or omitted altogether.

Stage 2. Professional trainers set standards

To get to stage 2 the organisation has to make a conscious decision to be more professional in the way it handles training. A restaurant chain might decide its customers expect a certain standard. So they train their waiting staff accordingly. It employs professionally qualified training staff, who know how to set training objectives. They also check the suitability of nominations for training but they would not have any systems in place, such as an evaluation or learning system (see Chapter 4). The trainers would, however, ask more questions than an administrator about training needs (eg do waiters need to know the ingredients of each item on the menu?) so they can design and deliver professional training programmes.

However, these professionals might not control the training budget. Also, because they have no systems in place to control training, line managers will normally be allowed to bypass the training team if they choose. A manager may choose to take their team away for a weekend team event without any involvement from their professional training function. Consequently, there is very little consistency in training provision. Also, the board are still more concerned at this stage about minimum standards than they are about seeking to achieve a competitive advantage through training. A subtle but crucial distinction.

We can also begin to consider the employee's perspective in more detail at this point. If their previous employer ran a small corner café, they will regard their current employer as progressive because they have a more professional approach to training. Despite this, most of the training they experience will be in the classroom on standard modules. Of course, today, some of these modules would be delivered through an e-learning portal but the use of this sort of technology does not automatically mean the organisation is any more mature. Calling it 'e-learning' does not mean the organisation understands the concept of 'learning' (see Chapter 7). If it is, in effect, just a case of delivering existing classroom content online it would be better described as e-training. The real motivation in using new technology for e-training is purely to reduce training costs, not enhance learning opportunities.

Perhaps the main point to note about stage 2 though is that a 'professional approach' only gets the organisation about a third of the way along the scale. The trainers and developers are still primarily *reacting*, to *perceived* training needs and they are in a role where they are regarded as 'servants to the line'. There is no sense of equality here. Only when they move onto stage 3 does their role really start to change.

Stage 3. Trainers become more effective

Stage 1 organisations jump to the conclusion that they need training and are not too concerned about what sort of training as long as it keeps them out of trouble. So a standard module on customer service might be the order of the day. Stage 2 organisations start to ask more questions, such as 'How do we make sure customer service training is of a high standard?' Trainers in stage 3 organisations ask very different questions altogether.

For a start, they have a training system in place that says no training will be provided unless a proper training needs analysis (TNA) has been undertaken. However, this only represents a more mature approach if they have already educated their organisation to believe that this is the way training should be carried out. Line managers will be expecting more searching questions from these trainers than they ever heard from the administrator. However, these managers have learned by now that having to answer the tough questions makes the training more effective. They also realise that effective training is in their interest, leading them to value their trainer's expertise rather than perceive them as asking too many awkward questions. Maturity is about managers and trainers working in harmony, not one side placing the other under duress.

Effective training managers undertake a proper TNA in order to identify *real* training needs. Through their analysis they reveal that some parts of the organisation already give great customer service and so conclude that they do not need any training in this subject. They also find that some of the customer service problems start right back in the warehouse; where despatch are sending out damaged products. They then focus part of their energy and resources on resolving some of these underlying problems, which they now refer to as root causes. Root cause analysis requires a bespoke training solution, so the warehouse manager now starts to understand what business-focused training looks like. An external observer will see the beginnings of a virtuous circle. Good practice leads to results and, in turn, even better practices. Not quite a nascent, learning organisation just yet though. Some managers will need further convincing that learning and organisational performance go hand-in-hand.

Word of mouth about the effectiveness of this new approach to training reaches the ears of senior managers and it would be nice to claim that they all suddenly now realise the benefits of training. If only life were that simple. We should not forget that stage 3 organisations are still relatively immature: they have a long way to go. Some senior managers can actually take a rather negative view because they perceive these developments as the training team trying to encroach onto their managerial territory. They will need more persuasive arguments to encourage them to buy in to a new style of training. To fully convince these people the whole organisation first has to jump the evaluation hurdle.

Evaluation hurdle

We will put evaluation into its conceptual and theoretical context in Chapter 3, but the main, practical consideration here is the attitude of senior managers. As we will see when we come to ROI, one purpose of evaluation is to express the real value of training and development, in £s, in order to gain the commitment of everyone in the organisation: managers and employees alike. Getting over this hurdle is *not* about collecting lots of data, it is about educating everyone that effective training is about constant feedback. Did the training work? If not, then why not? What can we learn from that experience? It is evaluation that will move the organisation from a narrow, blinkered view of 'training' to a concept of 'learning'. This represents the biggest shift in organisational maturity on this scale. It requires no less than a complete breakthrough in thinking and once this breakthrough is achieved the organisation will be transformed. Training is about inputs (eg putting people on courses), whereas learning is about outputs (ie what was the impact on the business of what they learned?). To ensure this shift happens the trainer now has to change their own role to that of a learning consultant.

Stage 4. The trainer becomes a learning consultant who acts as a business partner

The shift between stages 3 and 4 is huge and will take a considerable amount of time. It also necessitates the installation of an evaluation system (see Chapter 4 on systems) that incorporates the Baseline Model. In practice this means the customer service training is now really well designed. Not only does it focus on the parts of the business where it is really needed but measures of customer satisfaction will have already been collected as part of the re-vamped TNA process. Furthermore, this has been converted into potential lost sales and an ROI figure produced. It reflects an attractive potential return of 165 per cent in a clear and simple language the board understands.

In a stage 4 organisation managers do not expect to be offered standard, generic modules any more and they become accustomed to working with learning consultants. They appreciate the bespoke solutions they are offered because they have experienced the results (revealed through evaluation) and they talk about 'learning opportunities', not 'courses'. In fact, some of them are running regular team briefing meetings, facilitated by someone from the learning team, where they discuss how to improve the way they work and the learning consultant picks up on any areas requiring further support. Some of these will be delivered through the re-designed, just-in-time, e-learning portal.

Everything though is very structured and happens systematically. It is also very focused on the 'here-and-now' operational tasks and measures. This focus will gradually start to shift as the organisation continues to mature and enters into the transitional phase: stage 5.

Stage 5. Transition phase

The concept of learning is now well established and the use of feedback loops really does start to drill down into some serious organisational issues. There is a noticeable shift from single-loop to double-loop learning (see Chapter 6) which cuts across departments and functions. The rigid, silo organisation has had to flex to enable this to happen.

So, for example, if customer service is deteriorating is it because the products are defective or after-sales service is not resolving problems quickly and efficiently? The learning consultant will already have had some involvement in this issue because they already operate cross-functionally. Their new process analysis skills have enabled them to pinpoint where most of the problems lie. Some of these problems arise out of a conflict between what the product developers have produced, what the sales people offer and what the after-sales people can deliver. This can only be resolved by the three teams working together to reach a satisfactory solution.

This type of problem is obviously more prevalent in stage 1 organisations because they never learn. They are immature because no effective analysis takes place. Instead the simplistic answer is to send the teams, separately, on awaydays and team-building courses with no clear purpose. Stage 2 organisations also just organise awaydays for their teams but they do it more professionally. The learning consultant, on the other hand, has managed to help the organisation reach stage 5 maturity by establishing who the owner of the process is (eg head of product development). The head personally accepts responsibility and is ultimately accountable, but realises he or she has the authority to knock heads together if necessary. The learning consultant is operating at a higher level, with the power players.

Towards the end of this transition phase the organisation has learned that solving these problems is absolutely fundamental to the way the business operates and it informs their strategic thinking for the future design and development of the organisation. Only then can it hope to benefit from reaching the organisational learning stage.

Stage 6. Organisational learning

Although many people in HR and training circles have been talking about 'the learning organisation' for years there is little evidence that such entities exist. How can an organisation really attach sufficient weight to learning efforts if they have not been able to see the business benefits? They need to have experienced breaking through the evaluation hurdle. So, in the absence of a clear example of what a learning organisation might look like, here is one view of how achieving this level of maturity might feel.

At this stage learning that adds value is occurring continuously, quite naturally and almost unconsciously. A high level understanding of the concept of knowledge management means a knowledge-sharing environment exists (and has been created right back during the organisation design and recruitment phase). Employees are truly regarded as a pool of intellectual capital, with their innovative ideas being welcomed as a means of releasing their full potential. Finally, the organisation has managed to achieve that elusive 'not-seeking-to-blame' culture; an absolute prerequisite if the organisation really wants to describe itself as a learning organisation.

So if the whole of the Learning Maturity Scale is dependent on climbing, or even knocking down, the evaluation hurdle, we now need to examine this hurdle in much more detail. As we will soon see though, in order to defeat this hurdle we will have to go right back to the beginning. To the very purpose of training itself.

2 ■ PUTTING EVALUATION IN ITS PROPER CONTEXT

■ WHAT IS THE PURPOSE OF TRAINING?

The simplest and most fundamental question that evaluation asks is whether training achieved its intended purpose. To answer this question, of course, we must have a clear purpose in mind before we start to train. Yet in practice it is amazing how many 'purposes' training seems to acquire along the way. Here are just a few of them:

- 'I want him to go on this course as a thank you/pat on the back/reward for doing a good job.'
- 'People like training so it will help us with retention.'
- 'Training always boosts staff morale.'
- 'We're recognising her potential by putting her on the leadership programme.'
- 'He's been pestering me to get some training so anything for a quiet life.'
- 'I need that computer programming language on my cv.'

This list could be endless and the items might look like statements of purpose, but in fact none of them fulfil the primary purpose of organisational training and development.

Broadly speaking training can only have two purposes:

- mandatory training – that is, training the organisation *has* to do in order to bring employees up to a minimum standard or to ensure compliance with regulations or the law. This will include probationer training, induction, how to use the organisation's systems and basic product knowledge

and/or

- improvement training – that is, training that the organisation *chooses* to do to improve the performance of employees through more efficient or effective ways of working. This might include problem solving, sales techniques or training managers to manage their staff to obtain improved performance.

Both of these can be combined in one purpose statement for training:

> The purpose of training is to meet operational standards or to add value by raising individual and organisational performance levels.

Based on this definition none of the 'purposes' in the first list satisfy this definition. Yet it is obvious that a great deal of training has the sole purpose of meeting minimum standards (eg life insurance salespeople have to pass their FPC exams to satisfy the regulations). The other aspect of this definition though, the 'added value' purpose, can be represented graphically using a learning curve as shown in Figure 2.1

The learning curve is a concept that is easily understood by most employees. It starts very steeply (everyone experiences the 'steep learning curve' when they have to learn an enormous amount, quickly, on their first day in a new job). Gradually, though, the gradient of the curve becomes less steep with time (as they settle into the job) but it never actually levels off. There is always something new to learn. No one is perfect.

But Figure 2.1 is not just a learning curve. It includes the cost and revenue lines of the business (in a non-commercial organisation we might include cost and quality of service as the two key variables) and states, quite clearly and unequivocally, that the learning curve is a meaningless concept unless it is directly related to organisational

Figure 2.1 The learning curve means learning to improve the organisation

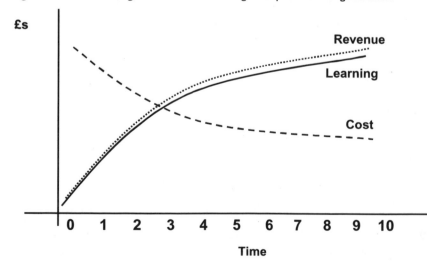

performance. If learning has no impact on revenue or cost it is worthless. Moreover, the causal connections between learning and performance should be as clear and direct as possible.

Some readers might already find some difficulty in accepting this basic proposition. Surely there is more to learning than simple cost and revenue, they might ask? Well, we will return to these two categories in more depth in Chapters 3 and 6 (especially when explaining the 3 Box System). However, regardless of the specific reasons, organisations generally invest in training because they believe it is worth it. It would be a bit stupid to invest in something if you did not think it was worth anything. However, they might not articulate this very openly or clearly. They certainly would rarely be specific about the financial return they would expect; regardless of whether they actually calculated the ROI or not (see Chapter 5). The logic seems very obvious, but what if the purpose of a particular piece of training is not so clear-cut?

Some trainers argue that training and development is about providing other 'intangible' benefits to the individual, such as personal growth or career development. Others would suggest that training has, in some way, a social responsibility and that learning can be an end in itself. Of course, the individual should benefit, personally, from learning, but is that the main purpose of training? Indeed, could we expect organisations to continue to spend money on training if they believed that there was no financial return to be gained?

It sounds as if the two objectives might actually be in conflict with each other: either the organisation will benefit or the individual, but not both. Maybe the key question here is: do business benefits and individual benefits have to be mutually exclusive? Certainly any trainer who thinks profit is a dirty word will struggle to justify their training expenditure unless they try to resort to a different type of indicator, perhaps like this one:

> ❝ Let's hear it for emotional, spiritual and personal satisfaction profit. ❞

This quote is from a contributor to a UK-based, training website (www.UKHRD.com), made during a debate about the use and relevance of ROI in training. Some contributors seemed to think that the purpose of training should not always be linked to hard, commercial factors, like profit. They suggested there were other advantages, such as spiritual benefits, to be had. Of course, training may well result in personal, spiritual enlightenment and it can often be fun, but these sorts of benefits are purely incidental. The icing on the cake, as it were. Evaluation is not about measuring how nice or how thick the icing is, but about checking how well training is delivering its primary function of both organisational and individual effectiveness.

However, this does not appear to sit very comfortably with the notion of 'learning to learn' that some organisations adopt as a policy. For them, any learning is good. Regardless of whether this is true or not, every time I pick up a newspaper, or watch a documentary on TV, or use the internet I do learn something. There is also a chance that some of what I learn might end up influencing what I do at work. But then much of what I learn, while of great interest to me, could be of little practical use. I might learn to speak French at night classes but never have reason to use it for the benefit of my organisation. Learning, from an organisation's viewpoint, is not an end in itself. Organisations really want learning and improvement to happen simultaneously even if they do not always declare that this is their aim.

It should also be pointed out that there is absolutely no reason why training for profit or value (which applies just as much to the not-for-profit sectors) should limit or detract from the many personal benefits that individuals receive from training and development. Indeed, learning and personal development should always be mutually inclusive. I would go even further and argue that a clear focus on organisational performance objectives, at the training design stage, not only produces the real £ value that we are seeking but it simultaneously enhances the learning experience for all concerned.

Even if training really does boost staff morale, because you are showing some interest in them, then we would hope that improved morale leads to improved productivity or even greater creativity. Learning has to be a win-win situation otherwise organisations will stop investing in it. I have yet to meet a CEO or finance director who, when asked the straight question 'Would you invest in training if you never received a return on your investment?', was prepared to say yes. Evaluation is about measuring that return.

Of course, you could follow the old adage that measuring a pig does not make it fat and argue that *measuring* the benefits of training, in itself, does not make the training beneficial. In other words, the process of evaluating does not improve the benefits, it just puts a number on them. As we will see from Chapter 3 onwards though, the process of evaluation will, itself, add enormous value to the learning process.

In fact, the evaluator needs to start from an assumption that there is *no* benefit from training until they have seen some results. Why? Because it is much easier than you might imagine for training to add no value whatsoever. Here are a few possible ways in which 'professional' training courses can fail to deliver any benefits:

■ the trainees did not learn anything new

■ the trainees were not motivated

- the programme was inappropriate

- they were made redundant or left the company straight after the training

- their boss didn't allow them to use what they learned when they returned to work

- the company collapsed.

Hopefully, none of these eventualities will happen, but training has to be designed on the basis that you want as high a probability as possible that the learning will be effective. Just assuming that it will have some benefit takes no account of the theory of probability. If you have never studied the theory of probability before, then this is a knowledge gap you need to fill.

LEARNING PROBABILITY

If you toss a coin there is an equal probability, or equal chance, that it will turn up either heads or tails (shown as a half, evens or 50:50 chance in Figure 2.2). It does not matter how many times it turns up heads or tails, on the next toss it still has an equal chance of either being heads or tails. However, probability theory tells us that if you toss it over, say, a million times the chances are that it will turn up heads roughly as often as it turns up tails.

Other ways of looking at probability theory are that if you drive down a motorway on the Friday evening before a Bank Holiday there is a much higher probability than usual that you will get stuck in traffic. Probability theory also tells us that on any given, normal Saturday, the shops will be busy but it is highly improbable (probably much less than ¼) that everyone will decide to go to the shops all at the same time.

So how does probability apply to training? Well, if you are running a customer service training programme you have to ask yourself 'What is the probability that the programme will actually result in improved customer service?' Figure 2.2 shows that if this was an absolute certainty then it would have a probability of 1. However, if the staff on the customer service programme had nothing to do with customer service then the probability would be zero: it would be impossible to improve customer service through

Figure 2.2 What is the probability of learning being effective?

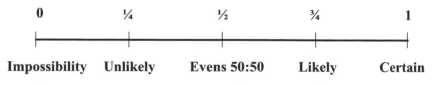

0	¼	½	¾	1
Impossibility	Unlikely	Evens 50:50	Likely	Certain

this training. In between these two extremes are a range of probabilities from very likely to very unlikely.

Based on this theory it is the job of the trainer to design their training in such a way that it ensures as high a level of probable success as possible. In order to do this think of all of the factors that need to be brought into consideration. What about the:

- clarity of the business objective (need) behind the training
- ability of the trainee to influence that objective
- motivation and commitment of the trainee
- motivation, commitment and ownership of the manager
- accuracy of the TNA
- method of design
- mode of delivery?

As we will see later, one of the key roles of the evaluation process is to aim to achieve the highest level of probability (and see Chapter 6). Evaluation does not attempt to 'prove' anything. It just tries to increase the chances of training spend producing the best possible return on investment.

We can easily see why the role of evaluation is so important if we examine what happens to training when no one bothers to introduce evaluation into the equation. Take a look at some of these findings from Dr Bruce Pfau, who works for the actuaries Watson Wyatt and is co-author of *The Human Capital Edge* (2001). He had researched the connection between HRM practices and business performance and when he was interviewed on www.HR.com on 3 February 2003 he remarked:

> ❝ The third most important finding, and perhaps the most controversial finding, is that some HR practices generate more value than others and some actually are associated with downturns in economic value. For example, multi-rater feedback is a questionable practice, and training aimed at helping employees advance to positions sometime in the future, rather than training aimed at more proximate needs, was also suspect. Finally, with unfocused HR service technologies — those whose goal is changing culture or freeing HR to do higher kinds of services — the results were associated with decreasing shareholder value. In contrast, HR technologies with a clear focus, such as increasing customer service or decreasing cost, create a lot of value. ❞

By multi-rater feedback Dr Pfau is referring to the very popular 360° feedback systems in use in many organisations. His findings suggest that not only do these fail to bring any benefits but they actually damage the organisation in terms of reduced value. Also, development activity that aims to produce suitable employees for positions 'sometime in the future' is not as effective as that which focuses more on the here and now. These are incredible findings. If they are correct then it completely undermines what many training and development teams are currently doing. When they take their eye off the ball (of results) they also lose sight of the goal. They only fall into this trap, however, because they have failed to follow a discipline of evaluation. They are guilty of assuming that such unfocused training is bound to achieve some results.

TRAINING IS GUILTY UNTIL PROVEN INNOCENT

All the books I have ever read on evaluation seem to make one fundamental error, right at the start. They make an implicit assumption that training is always bound to produce some benefit, however small. If you accept this assumption then you might only view evaluation as a means of measuring the size of this assumed benefit. So a leadership development programme is assumed to be beneficial and the evaluator tries to work out *how* beneficial. This might seem quite logical but the problem with this stance is that it presupposes all training is good and the only consequent question is 'how good?'

If you follow this logic and assume all training will produce an acceptable return on investment (let us say a 30 per cent net return) then you should be investing every £ you have in training instead of other business investments that cannot match this return. Of course this apparent 'logic' is nonsense. As they say in the financial services industry 'investments can go down as well as up' so wise choices have to be made. Training should never be given a blank cheque.

It is also a very narrow and limited view of the purpose of evaluation and the many other potential advantages it brings. The starting point adopted for the purposes of this book is entirely different: in fact it takes the completely opposite view. Our basic assumption will be that there is no benefit from training until an evaluation process produces some evidence of such benefits. In effect, training is guilty until proven innocent: guilty of using scarce organisational resources until such time as it can justify the expenditure.

Now this is not a text book and neither is it an academic work, although it certainly contains important elements of both. It is a book for practitioners and pragmatists. That does not mean it is anything less than totally professional. Having a solid understanding of the theories of training, learning and evaluation is absolutely critical for anyone who wants to call himself or herself a 'learning professional'. If you do not understand the theory then your practice is more than likely to be highly suspect.

But even if you do understand the theory there will be many other pressures and influences tempting you to disregard it and compromise whenever it seems expedient. Managers often want instant solutions and quick fixes because they are too busy to allow enough time for planning. So this book tries to suggest how to get the best of both worlds. It will encourage you to stick to the theory as much as possible whilst always offering the most practical and pragmatic learning solutions to any problems you are likely to encounter. So let us at least make an attempt to ensure that we all agree and understand what the basic theory of training is before we go any further.

THE CLASSICAL TRAINING CYCLE

The theory of training is based on a classic training cycle that is well accepted throughout the world and is shown in Figure 2.3. Most experienced trainers know and understand this cycle so well that they will be inclined to skip this bit. That would be a serious mistake because the reason most trainers have a problem with evaluation is:

a they do not fully understand all the implications of this cycle

b they do not follow the cycle in practice.

They know that before they decide to offer any training solutions they should undertake a through training needs analysis (TNA). Once they know what training is required (eg the administrators need to know how to use Word for word processing) they can *design* a programme and *deliver* it by whatever means they deem most appropriate (eg classroom, book, online). Then they get to the *evaluation* step and, in this case, it would probably involve producing a sample document in Word, such as a letter, to prove that the administrators had learned the necessary skills and knowledge.

You will have noticed though that Figure 2.3 is drawn as a circle or cycle. This is quite intentional, as the key element of the cycle is a *feedback loop* and the cycle is meant to be a *closed loop* system. In other words, the training cycle is only complete when you have checked (evaluated) that the training achieved what it set out to achieve. We will see throughout this book though that the concept of cycles is a very common theme in training and learning.

This is certainly how the Classical Cycle was explained to me as a young training manager on my professional 'train the trainer' qualification course many years ago. When described in this way it seems so simple, especially if you only refer to a basic piece of word processing training. However, another way to describe the TNA phase of

Figure 2.3 The Classical Training Cycle

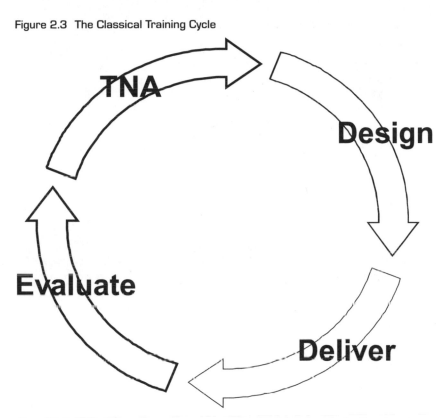

the training cycle is to refer to it as an organisational 'gap' analysis. So what do we mean by 'gap'? What sort of gaps are we referring to?

THERE ARE ONLY TWO TYPES OF TRAINING GAP

If you look at Figure 2.4 the Classical Training Cycle is now shown as a series of four steps with two possible routes to follow. The left-hand route shows that the organisation has a gap between the skills and knowledge it needs in order to produce letters efficiently and those currently possessed by its workforce. Consequently it demands that every employee should know how to use Word.

In this simple case the answer is to design a standard course to teach all the key features of Word required to produce a letter (eg page setup, fonts, bold, underlining, etc). The 'evaluation' of this training (more accurately described as 'validation', as we will see later) is then just a matter of asking employees who have completed the course to produce a test letter. You might find that up to as much as 75 per cent of training falls into this category.

Figure 2.4 Training or business gap

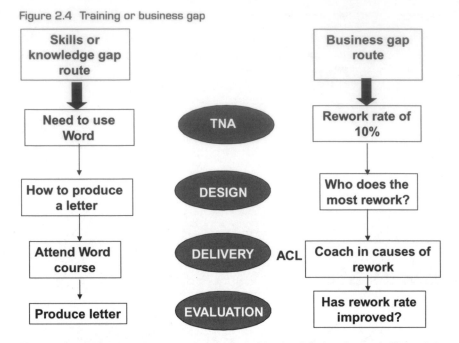

The rest should fall into the category represented by the right hand route in Figure 2.4: the business gap route. Here the gap has an obvious £ sign attached. In other words, the business is not achieving as high a revenue or as low a cost as it needs. In this case, costs are too high because of reworking (eg having to resend documents, or repair or amend parts in some way). However, if you look at the design phase this now reveals the gap as a *performance* gap – some teams are doing more rework than others and this needs to be resolved through coaching the team leaders who have particular problems. You will notice that this is much more like an ACL (action centred learning) approach, rather than delivering a 'rework course'. Again the evaluation phase (this time real evaluation because of the £ sign) is relatively simple because the original rework rate is now re-measured.

So if all trainers accept that the classical training cycle, with evaluation, is a fundamental building block of effective training, why do they not always follow it? Well, part of the reason is that busy managers do not always allow trainers the time to follow the cycle properly, but there are at least three more fundamental reasons.

It only works for simple training

As soon as you try to apply the training cycle to something more complex than Word training or a simple rework problem (management development for example) the Classic Cycle just does not cope very well. How do you analyse management development needs at the TNA stage? The conventional way is to analyse skills (eg the ability to plan and organise) and, to a lesser extent, behaviours (eg listening). Many trainers these days also try to analyse competencies but we can immediately see that these are not as easy to pin down as the knowledge of 'How to use page setup in Word', or as easy to demonstrate.

Nevertheless, this does not stop organisations and their training departments from wanting to run management development programmes. Regardless of whether they pin down specific skills needs or not, we can all see and feel what it is like working with managers who are in need of some improvement. We recognise, quite easily, that they are disorganised or give unclear or conflicting instructions. So the desire to improve this situation is probably a valid one. Unfortunately, though, converting the need into a measurable improvement, through training and development, is another matter entirely.

Moreover, spotting non-specific or general management problems tends to encourage development professionals, particularly, to fall into another trap that arises out of a misunderstanding of the Classic Cycle.

TNA means individual TNA

The training needs analysis stage of the cycle was always intended to analyse the training needs of a particular *individual*. This point seems to have been missed in recent years in the way trainers are trained. The whole point of having individual appraisals and personal development reviews was that individual needs would be addressed. This would generally be regarded as best practice in training and development.

However, the reality in many organisations is that modern trainers just skip the TNA stage altogether or replace it with what can only be termed a *generic* TNA. They decide what a good manager looks like, and all the skills such a manager is likely to need, and then produce the programmes to suit. Everything is broken down into a series of stand-alone modules on subjects such as delegation, negotiation, even project management. Alongside these will be some 'soft skills' development such as 'interpersonal skills'. This might look like a TNA but it is really more like a training and development wish list: 'Wouldn't it be fantastic if every manager had these skills? So let's put them all through such a programme.'

No attempt is made here to address individual needs, but the training team now have a menu of ready-made training programmes, which hard-pressed managers can use during appraisal to select training for their staff. This might appear to make the lives of both the line manager and the development manager easier in the short term but it is definitely a case of putting the cart before the horse. This was never the intention behind the classical theory of training.

In more recent years this approach has become almost the new orthodoxy. With the advent of competence frameworks, based on the notion of generic sets of competencies possessed by high-performing managers, many developmental programmes have been designed and delivered with little, if any, tailoring to real individual needs. Look at this comment on UKHRD (19 March 2004) from a training and development manager in a Japanese electronics company:

> **❝** The modus operandi of the programme is that we will produce pools of future leaders from which the best candidates will be selected when the role becomes vacant. A lot of work has already been done around producing the required competences for future leaders and scoping out the required development, so I am happy that we have this covered. However, there are a couple of characteristics that we believe are key to the success of the programme that we still have to tie down. These are:– 1. How we select the best candidates .... **❞**

Somehow this manager seems to have managed to get the whole process the wrong way round (and there are not even any existing vacancies for any suitable candidates). This seems to be a good example of what Dr Pfau unearthed. Long-term development plans with no clear objective.

Who knows whether any of this activity will work or not? Well, the theory of the Classic Cycle should tell us the answer. You will only ever know what works if you evaluate it. In the case of competencies this usually involves some assessment of competence development including tools such as 360° feedback systems (although these were also criticised by Dr Pfau). Do your subordinates, colleagues and peers feel that your managerial competence has improved? As we will see in Chapter 3 though, whether this really constitutes a proper evaluation is open to question.

One thing can be said with absolute certainty. The TNA and evaluation stages of the cycle are inextricably linked. TNA is to evaluation what the doctor's diagnosis is to a healthy patient. The needs identified become the criteria for evaluation. If the needs are indistinct the evaluation is equally indistinct and you may never know whether the patient is getting better or not.

TNA was never a simple process. In fact it is probably the most skilful part of a trainer's job. But anyone who thinks the TNA stage is difficult without evaluation will have even greater difficulties when they get three-quarters of the way around the cycle and try to evaluate their management development programmes. It is only then that you have to close the loop and demonstrate that these same managers have improved the skills that the training was designed for in the first place.

The more you think about this the more you have to come to the conclusion that maybe we need to be thinking about the evaluation stage at the same time as we are undertaking the needs analysis. Perhaps, in effect, we should move the position of evaluation in the cycle?

Evaluation is in the wrong place

One thing we have not mentioned yet about the training cycle is: where does it start? It was always assumed that the obvious place to start would be the TNA. If you are sitting down with a manager to discuss the training needs of their team the most obvious place to start would appear to be the question 'What training do your people need?' Unfortunately this is one of many misconceptions surrounding the training cycle. It might sound counter-intuitive but the place to start the cycle is actually at the point we would normally regard as the end of the cycle – at the evaluation phase.

What do I mean by this? Well, the first question to a line manager should not be 'What training do your people need?' but rather 'What business objectives can you not achieve without some training and development?' These might both sound like the same question but the former identifies a training objective while the latter a business objective. A subtle but crucial distinction.

THE NEO-CLASSICAL TRAINING CYCLE

If the manager's answer is 'I cannot raise customer satisfaction levels without effective training' then any subsequent training can only be evaluated against this criterion. So maybe the Classic Cycle should always have emphasised that the evaluation questions come into the cycle twice: once at the beginning (what is the business need?) and once at the end (was this business need satisfied?). These questions set up the loop and close it. What customer satisfaction levels do you want and then, afterwards, what customer service levels were achieved? So now we have a slightly amended version of the Classic Cycle. Perhaps we should, therefore, call it the Neo-Classical Training Cycle, as shown in Figure 2.5

Of course, for any trainer using the Neo-Classical Cycle they will need to understand their business's needs much better than a trainer who only wants to design and deliver generic training programmes. The Neo-Classical Cycle also assumes that the line manager is willing to allow the training needs analyst to ask possibly awkward questions about how they and their team are performing. This would be too big an assumption.

Figure 2.5 The Neo-Classical Cycle starts and ends with evaluation

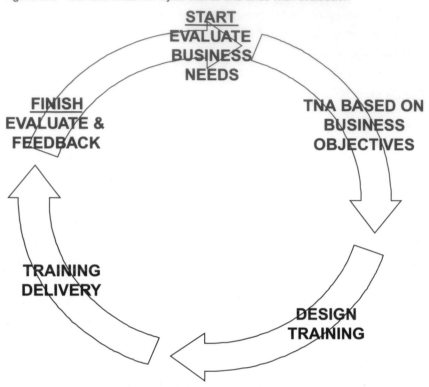

START
EVALUATE
BUSINESS
NEEDS

TNA BASED ON
BUSINESS
OBJECTIVES

FINISH
EVALUATE &
FEEDBACK

DESIGN
TRAINING

TRAINING
DELIVERY

This is where events and practical considerations test the Cycle and reveal how easily and quickly it may be discarded. If you are faced with an immature organisation (stage 1 on the Learning Maturity Scale) then your line managers will be used to getting whatever training they request. They may not want to spend too long in the discussions on underlying business needs that the Neo-Classical Cycle demands. Consequently it is not too difficult to understand why trainers in these circumstances so easily make compromises. Despite their best efforts to adhere to a cycle that they know is correct, when a senior manager asks 'Can't you just put together a customer service course for me?' they often do their best to please, still acting as a servant to the line.

Nevertheless, every time such a compromise is made, the basic foundation for effective training is undermined. If a trainer agrees to design a customer service programme just because a manager asks for one, then in effect, by their own admission, they have just completely ignored what their own professional code dictates. As a direct consequence of failing to stick to the rules the resulting training is bound to be less effective. Otherwise why bother having the rules at all?

The trainer's defence of expediency might resolve his or her immediate problem of delivering what the manager wants, but how much respect would you have for a 'professional' who does not even stick to their own principles? We should not be surprised, therefore, when training subsequently fails to attract the attention it deserves in the boardroom. Putting evaluation in the right place and with the right emphasis presents us with the greatest opportunity yet to remedy this fundamental deficiency and to ensure training finds its rightful position in organisational management and continuous performance improvement.

3 ■ EVALUATION – THE THEORY

In Chapter 2 we put evaluation in its rightful place, at the very heart of training theory, by showing that its correct position within the training cycle is at the beginning. Now we need to examine the theory of evaluation itself. Again, you might be tempted to want to skip the theory and to concentrate on the more practical aspects of this book in Part 2. However, you might be surprised to find that the theory of evaluation presented here is very different to anything you might have studied in the past. Nevertheless, this theory is likely to be a great deal easier to understand than you might fear and, when you do possess a full understanding, you will be able to deal, confidently, with any training evaluation issue in any set of circumstances.

So let us begin by looking at the three key elements in the theory of evaluation:

■ its purpose – what exactly is evaluation meant to do?

■ the need for an evaluation model – or a set of steps to follow and

■ the need for an evaluation system – to work in conjunction with the model as a model, in its own right, is not enough to do evaluation in practice

Just before we look at these in detail, though, we need to remove a particularly old and troublesome red herring – the question of attributability.

■ THAT OLD RED HERRING – ATTRIBUTABILITY

Many of the trainers who come to workshops and conferences on the subject of evaluation are reluctant to learn. They say it is not worth evaluating because it is impossible to attribute a specific business result to a specific piece of training. Such trainers want to avoid evaluation at all costs. They usually voice their objections in the form of a question such as 'How will you prove that it's the training that's making the difference?' or 'How can you isolate the impact of training from all the other factors and variables that come into play?'

There are several ways to deal with these objections. First, evaluation is not really meant to be about grabbing some credit for the training department. So trying to prove, beyond all doubt, that training had a specific impact is not the main issue.

Second, no department or function can actually claim that any business result is down to their own specific efforts. The sales team cannot prove that sales have gone up just because they are so good at selling, nor can the marketeer claim it was because their advertising campaign was so brilliant. What about the product design team who designed a brilliant product in the first place or even the production team who managed to keep the price down? Organisations where departments fight to claim sole credit for results or vie with each other for the accolades are very immature.

So, instead of becoming bogged down trying to prove who contributed what, let us take a step back and ask what evaluation is meant to reveal.

THE PURPOSE OF EVALUATION

Evaluation should not be a chore. Neither should it be used to measure every bit of potential benefit from learning. Some trainers think it is not worth bothering with evaluation unless the result is perfect. This seems to me to be an odd stance to take. That if you cannot attain perfection it is not worth trying. Imagine asking any prospective parent if they can think of any reason not to have children. The chances are they could come up with many reasons (especially if they have any experience of teenagers!) but, even with the benefit of hindsight, none of these negative considerations would have made them decide not to have children. Just because results are not perfect does not mean we should not try. One of John Harvey Jones' favourite sayings was 'best is the enemy of good'. Evaluation has an enormous contribution to make without having to provide a perfect measure.

Evaluation is not an attempt to prove that training is working. It is not even the last act in the training cycle. *It is an integral part of the way individuals and organisations learn to improve.* We can show this by reference to two other famous cycles: the PDCA Cycle and Kolb's Learning Cycle.

In Figure 3.1 the PDCA cycle (normally associated with the quality guru Deming, although more accurately attributed to the work of Walter Shewart as far back as the 1920s) is predicated on having pre-measures which you then *plan* to improve. The *check* stage (or 'evaluate' in training terms) tells you whether things are improving or not. A

Figure 3.1 Deming and Kolb – the same theory with an emphasis on evaluation

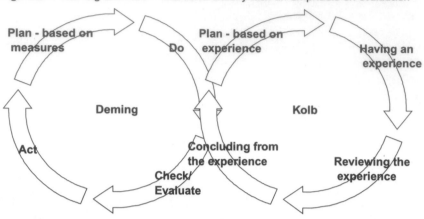

simple example would be to measure the number of complaints received then to do something to reduce them.

In contrast, a simple reading of Kolb's Learning Cycle refers to reviewing one's experiences. This is where an individual evaluates their own experience before drawing any conclusions (or learning) from it. Imagine that the person measuring the complaints learns that 90 per cent of them emanate from one department. Their immediate action might be to sit down with the head of that department to discuss this issue. In effect, they transfer their own learning to the workplace but also focus it on a priority.

The PDCA is about organisational improvement. Kolb is about individual learning. They are, in effect, both describing exactly the same cyclical process and together make an incredibly powerful combination, practically as well as conceptually, as we will see in Chapter 6. As a composite cycle they constitute a cycle for organisational learning. Hence we can now define the purpose of evaluation as being:

> To help individuals to *learn* how to *improve* the *effectiveness* of their *organisation*

Each of the words highlighted is crucial in this statement of purpose. Evaluation is about *learning*, but learning is meaningless unless it means *improvement*. What sort of improvement are we seeking? Well the only thing that matters is how *effective* the *organisation* is as a whole. However, we will now start to refer to effectiveness as value, or added value, a concept that will become crucial in evaluation.

When defined in this way evaluation can achieve many things. It can:

- align all training and development with business needs through the gap analysis undertaken at the beginning of the training cycle

- increase the commitment to training from both a manager and the 'trainee' because they will see training as mutually beneficial in helping them and the organisation to learn and perform better as a result.

- feedback results, good as well as bad, so that everyone can learn from the experience

- motivate by highlighting an individual's contribution to organisational effectiveness

- help to prioritise training expenditure (ie the biggest gaps will attract the most resources)

- act as a basis for a system of continuous improvement because of its inherently cyclical, iterative nature.

In view of all of this, it is actually quite easy to make a case for putting more effort into the evaluation phase of the training cycle. But to turn the theory of evaluation into practice we now need a practical model that will help us apply evaluation to any type of learning intervention. This means the actual choice of model now becomes critical, so what are the models on offer?

THE FAMOUS KIRKPATRICK MODEL

We could now review all of the different evaluation models that have been produced over the last 30 years or so, but there is an awfully large number of them. If such a review is of interest to you then look at Appendix 2, which briefly deals with this specific issue. However, one model, for better or worse, which has outlasted all the others is that developed by Donald Kirkpatrick in the US as far back as 1959, but made popular in the early 1970s. No other model is so well known or so often quoted and the vast majority of training professionals, if they use an evaluation model at all, would say they use Kirkpatrick's. So let us take Kirkpatrick as our jumping-off point and see whether it captures the essence of the theory of evaluation. In particular, does it point us towards any particular rules, laws of evaluation or a series of steps that have to be followed in practice?

Kirkpatrick identified his fundamental perspectives of evaluation in his four-level model (see Figure 3.2): reaction (level 1), testing (2), transfer of learning to the workplace (3) and results (4). When Kirkpatrick talks about testing at level 2, though, he always refers to

Figure 3.2 Kirkpatrick's four-level model

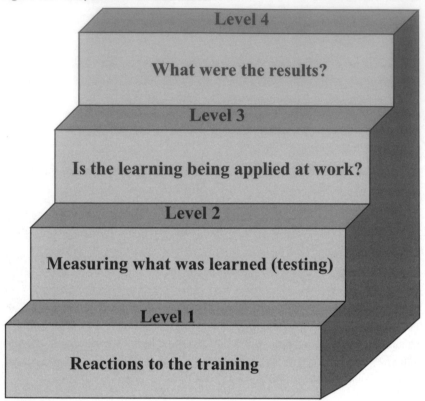

pre-tests as well. He always knew that trainees should be given a test, *before they are trained*, to find out how much they already know. They should then be given the same test, after the training is completed, to see if they know any more. He has, in effect, always followed the concept of pre-measurement enshrined in the PDCA Cycle yet this is rarely, if ever, spelled out when anyone refers to using Kirkpatrick's Model. So the real Kirkpatrick Model, even in its original form, should actually be shown with five levels, with pre-test, or what we will now call the trainee's 'baseline score', being the first level, as follows:

The real, five-level, Kirkpatrick model

    baseline – pre-training test scores

1   reaction

2   post-training test scores

3   transfer (or behaviour change)

4   organisational results.

Although Kirkpatrick fully acknowledged the baseline principle, he did not follow through on its full implications when he developed his theory. He did not make the baseline measures indispensable and so stopped short of producing a complete approach or methodology. In practice this means that any trainer, under the misapprehension that Kirkpatrick is just a four-level model, could be forgiven for thinking that evaluation can only start at level 1, that is, after the training has already happened. As we now know, this is already too late in the learning cycle and is precisely where the vast majority of problems in evaluation arise.

Another cause of serious problems in evaluation though is a complete misunderstanding of level 4.

What level 4 really means

The only way to e-*valu*-ate training is to show its true 'value', which, funnily enough, is what the word means. Value is a very simple concept and has a clear meaning. Kirkpatrick's references to level 4 'results' or 'organisational impact' do not really capture the essence of 'value' because they are too vague. The only way to add value to any organisation is to raise its income/revenue or reduce its costs (although we will look at the concept and practice of adding value in much more detail in Chapter 6). Improvements in both revenue and costs manifest themselves with clear £ signs. Even if we raise productivity levels or improve quality the ultimate effect is the same: an increase in either sales or margin (the difference between income and cost). There is no escaping this simple truth. Developing a senior manager's emotional intelligence means absolutely nothing if it is not translated into value. Having a happier workforce is only worth something if it means they are more productive, creative or innovative and this, in turn, delivers higher income or reduced costs.

Kirkpatrick never spelled this point out so he did not apply this simple, but very rigorous, test to his own version of level 4. That is why his model was never really an evaluation model: it never really focused on value. Instead, it can be regarded as primarily a training *validation* model. It looks mainly at training outcomes, not business outcomes. So, product knowledge training might result in an increase in product knowledge but a level 4 question about what value has been added seeks to establish whether that knowledge was put to good use and resulted in higher profits.

Kirkpatrick himself, of course, would take issue with me on this, and has done so when we have appeared on the same conference platform; pointing out that he has sales improvement figures after training to show his model does produce real £ signs. However, to do so he has to follow his own principle of measuring baseline sales figures *before* the programme started. This is such an obvious and unshakeable principle that it could be referred to as the first rule or even *law* of evaluation. In fact it is so important that only the word law gives it sufficient weight.

THE LAWS OF EVALUATION

Every academic discipline tends to have its own ground rules or 'givens'. As a young student of economics many years ago one of the first 'rules of the game' I had to learn were the laws of supply and demand and how these two forces came into equilibrium through the price mechanism. These laws are quite easy to understand but university library shelves are still stacked high with books that refine and further develop the theory that explains and underpins these laws. None of these books aim fundamentally to change the laws of supply and demand: there is only one set of laws.

It is also worth noting that no one invented these laws: they are *natural* laws. Anyone can easily see that human beings buy more of a product when the price drops and less when it increases. The theory of supply and demand is an attempt to explain this automatic, natural, human tendency. Economics, just like training, development and learning, is a social science that tries to understand, predict and even guide human behaviour.

So if training, development and learning are subject to certain universal laws, to what extent has the theory to underpin these laws been fully developed? In particular, how well developed is the theory of evaluation and should there be more than one model or set of laws? Moreover, if sound practice has to be based on sound theory, does Kirkpatrick's Model offer a sufficiently solid and robust foundation for both theory and practice? To check this we need to re-visit Kirkpatrick, in some detail, by working through a simple example. Then we can consider whether and how his model might need to be modified to make it more workable for the training practitioner.

TESTING KIRKPATRICK BY EVALUATING LANGUAGE TUITION

Imagine you want to teach an employee to speak a foreign language such as Spanish and you want to evaluate the impact this has. Following the basic principle of pre-training measures we could ask the students to take a test before they start their tuition classes. This might only tell us that they know just a few words in Spanish and therefore we could expect to see a significant improvement through the tuition.

Nevertheless, when we come to evaluate the tuition, provided the reactions (level 1) are very favourable; the trainees pass their follow-up, post-tuition Spanish test (level 2);

and we observe them using Spanish at work (level 3) one should have a level of confidence that this training is having the desired impact. But do any of these levels tell us anything about the real business impact? Is any of this data a true *evaluation*?

Kirkpatrick's Model suggests that only level 4 results will answer the *ultimate* question about the difference Spanish tuition has made to the business. But how do you get level 4 data? How about asking all of your Spanish-speaking customers whether they are doing more business with you and whether this was due to the fact that you now have staff who can speak Spanish? Even if you managed to get a customer to admit this it would be very tenuous and unconvincing.

It is worth considering now how you managed to get yourself into this situation? Well the reason you have to ask them now, after the training has already taken place, is because no one bothered to ask them before. No one had asked customers whether they would do more business with you if they could meet Spanish-speaking staff. So no level 4 objective was set in advance. No one actually predicted how much more business this training might generate. In effect, you end up trying to 'post-justify' training that had no pre-determined, level 4, targets set. This training could therefore be described, quite justifiably, as unfocused and poorly designed.

There is a much simpler way to deal with this issue though: make sure the business objectives (sales) behind the training need (speaking Spanish) are crystal clear, right from the start.

For example, what sort of Spanish language did you need? Conversational, technical or for legal documents? Was there really a business objective behind this training or was it just a nice idea that more employees should be bi-lingual? Practically speaking, there are only two reasons why this training might have been necessary (leaving aside the possibility that you could have recruited Spanish speakers or used agency interpreters and translators when necessary). One is to ask whether the Spanish tuition is a business *critical* activity. That is, will the business not be able to operate properly without it (eg airlines, where pilots are unable to fly without a knowledge of English) or will you be exposed to unnecessary risks without Spanish tuition (eg a misunderstood legal instruction or contractual term in Spanish)?

The second possibility is that the business might perform better as a direct result of the Spanish tuition. For example, what level of business is currently being achieved through your Spanish customers and what difference might improved language skills make? If this is the business objective that you opt for then you need to decide whether you want to work out what it might be worth in £s of extra sales.

In the real-life case of a merger between two engineering businesses in the 1990s (the UK-based GEC and the French-based Alsthom) a decision was taken that English would be the working language. However, English employees were encouraged and supported to learn to speak French. Regardless of the cost of this, in time and money, the business objectives behind the scheme were never entirely clear. Was it genuinely meant to help the business perform or was it just a nice idea that might enhance internal Anglo/French management relations? Was it a priority or did no one really care what the objective was? If the feedback sheets indicate that everyone enjoyed learning French and some of them used it for conversational purposes should that not be justification enough?

In this particular case the reality was that it was never seen as business critical, nor was it designed with any specific improvement measures in mind. It was just a nice idea. Yet, therein lies a fundamental organisational problem. Language tuition might not be the most important piece of training they ever did but the absence of a robust attitude to evaluation is a very serious issue. It is self-evident that if training is not *designed* to achieve business results there is a high probability that it will not produce any. One principle of measurement is that 'what gets measured gets done'; measurement drives behaviour. The converse of this argument is that anything left unmeasured attracts no priority. No evaluation means no measurement and no one will take ownership for training if no one is going to bother to measure the results. So what happens when attempts are made to train employees in risk avoidance, health and safety or problem-solving skills? If these are greeted with total indifference because no one is producing any measurements the organisation is leaving itself open to serious risks and also missing many opportunities for improvements.

So what can we learn from this? Well, the clarity with which success criteria for level 4 are defined (eg our Spanish customers should do more business with us) and the measures attached (we hope for a 1 per cent improvement in Spanish sales), in *advance* of any training, is bound to influence the whole learning process; both at the individual and organisational levels. Those who thought learning Spanish was fun now have to be committed to making it applicable in the workplace. Line managers who have targets to increase their sales in Spanish speaking markets will see the training as integral to their plans and efforts. In this way the very process of evaluation itself, starts to influence employee behaviour in line with organisational objectives.

We keep coming back to the same issue of pre-measurement as a critical part of the evaluation process. However, some things are more difficult to measure than others and this is where most readers will need some help. Defining business objectives can be quite tricky at the best of times and now we are saying that any business objectives agreed have to be as specific and as measurable as possible. The only way to achieve this effectively is to ask a well-structured series of questions that force the customers of training to be absolutely specific about their needs and the purpose of any subsequent training solution.

'BASIC' AND 'ADDED' VALUE

The first of these questions is 'What type of training do you want to do?' We referred earlier in Chapter 2 to a distinction between 'mandatory' and 'improvement' training. We then refined and developed this idea further in the language tuition example by asking how critical the training was. Now we can start to make a simpler and even clearer distinction between the two types of training (business critical or improvement), by linking them to two different value statements:

1 basic (or intrinsic) value and

2 added value.

You will soon see how this conceptual distinction is of paramount importance, not only in training evaluation and organisational learning theory but also, and more importantly, in terms of a practical, evaluation methodology.

Basic value

First, what do we mean by basic or intrinsic value? All organisations work to a set of standards, some implicit and some explicit, and the standards that an organisation sets for itself directly reflect their values. Hotels that do not regularly set a high standard of cleanliness are, in effect, making it clear that they do not value cleanliness. It also suggests that they think their customers do not value it either. Hence we see tables not cleared in the restaurant and ashtrays not emptied.

At the other end of the scale, however, the themed restaurant chain, TGI Friday, used to regard the minimum training standard for their waiting staff as being a complete knowledge of every ingredient, of every item, on their menu.

Now it would be virtually impossible for the management at TGI Friday to *prove* that this was necessary in order for them to run their business successfully. But does that really matter? As long as senior managers subscribe to a belief system that customers are prepared to pay for this level of service they will not be seeking any proof. Many successful businesses are run intuitively or follow similar articles of faith; they just presume that their customers demand certain standards and know that they have to meet those standards if they want to stay in business. In other words 'basic value' in business means survival.

But why is this so important in training evaluation? Because the impact or 'value' of the waiters' knowledge of the menu (and therefore the training required to achieve this standard of knowledge) is taken as read by the business. That is why they see no need to produce level 4 evaluation measures to justify the money spent. Instead, provided they can validate that it is having the desired impact at levels 2 and 3 (ie the waiters actually remember the menu to the required detail and they answer customers' questions accurately) then the actual value of the training to the business, in sales terms, is assumed to have been achieved. That is, customers like this level of detailed knowledge and come back again for this high standard of service; they see this as one way to differentiate between competing restaurant chains.

Basic value training generally tends, itself, to be pretty basic. Learning items on a menu is not rocket science and neither is it that interesting, but it has to be done and it has to be done well. Fortunately it presents few practical problems from an evaluation perspective but then its potential for adding much value is very limited. It only keeps the organisation operating at its most basic level.

For example, basic nursing training merely provides sufficient nursing skills to keep hospitals in operation. It does nothing to improve patient care or reduce the incidence of disease. Basic accounting means producing accounts, it does not guarantee profitability. So basic value can be viewed as treading water; there is no sense of progress, innovation or continuous improvement. The only way to attach a £ sign to this category of training is to ask the question 'How efficiently is it delivered? How much does it cost us to bring an employee up to the minimum standard required (say £200) and could we reach that same standard more cheaply (say, £100)?'

Not surprisingly few companies either want to or can afford merely to tread water. They want to start swimming as far and as fast as they can. This requires training that is designed with the specific and clear purpose of making an *additional* impact on the bottom line, over and above a basic level of operation. This comes under the heading of *added value*.

Added value

Value is *added* when the organisation *improves* over and above its normal level of operation. It is this shift or improvement that provides the basis for a true level 4 evaluation. It has all three key ingredients for evaluation:

- a start point (current performance)
- an end point (improved performance) and
- a £ sign (extra profit on sales).

If TGI Friday wanted to *improve* their business, by training their waiters to give an even better service, then the success criteria would have to be measured in terms of the increased sales that will arise from repeat business, customer recommendations or simply higher transaction values on drinks and meals.

But this is not meant to be only a hypothetical exercise. If the chosen measure for evaluation purposes is customer recommendations then someone has to start pre-measuring them (by asking customers if they came on a recommendation) and produce a snapshot of the existing situation (eg 20 per cent of existing customers were recommended to try TGI Friday). However, the only value measurement will be the £ sign attached to these figures so that, for example, if they:

a   currently have a total of 2 million customers per annum and this increases by 1 per cent (ie 20,000) because of extra recommendations and

b   the net profit margin on an average transaction is worth £3 per person then

c   the total added value is equal to £60,000 (a x b) per annum, on the bottom line.

The figures above are just for illustrative purposes but it is worth noting here that when calculations were actually made at TGI Friday in the UK on the relative performance of individual waiting staff the epos (electronic point of sale) system was sufficiently sophisticated for the improved performance of individual waiters/waitresses to be tracked. This enabled *individual* added value to be calculated in £s profit: a very interesting figure. As a direct consequence, a comparison was made between the relative performances of new and experienced staff so that a real £ value could be put on staff turnover (because turnover of more experienced staff leads to a greater loss of sales and customer satisfaction). One result of these calculations was that it could be demonstrated that a new waiter/waitress had to be retained for eight months before the company had recouped their initial recruitment and training costs through the profit they generated.

This, in turn, made the business reconsider their current policies on attracting and retaining staff. The individual value figures were presented to restaurant managers in order for them to take greater ownership of the problem of high staff turnover instead of regarding it as just an inevitable consequence of working in the restaurant industry. Restaurant managers could now see that showing little interest in new staff or treating them with minimal respect was costing them dearly. When these managers could see a direct, causal connection between training, turnover and their own restaurant's bottom line performance they naturally took much more of a personal interest in easing new employees into the business and ensuring they were developed properly. Hence the evaluation process itself had a profound effect on both organisational learning and operational management. Which is exactly what it should be designed to do.

CONCENTRATING EVERYONE ON LEVEL 4 TRANSFORMS THE LEARNING PROCESS

In practice it is relatively easy to design a learning intervention once a clear, level 4 business measure has been specified, so all trainers should be able to manage this. Yet really convincing level 4 evaluations are very rare in practice simply because trainers do not normally specify their level 4 criteria at the design stage. Even when trainers are taught the rules of evaluation there is still a reluctance to adopt pre-measurement as good training practice. This is due partly to a widely held belief that it is impossible to isolate a particular business result from a specific piece of training from all of the many other factors and variables that can come into the equation (eg changing market conditions, new competitors, new products, marketing campaigns etc). This is, of course, just an excuse (as was explained in Chapter 3). Some measures may be difficult to collect and yes, there are many variables that could influence the situation, but this does not invalidate the fundamental principle, established by Kirkpatrick, that pre-measurement is the only place to start in evaluation.

It might also be worth reminding ourselves again at this point why we would want to apply a robust evaluation model in the first place. It was stated earlier in this chapter, quite unequivocally, that the purpose of evaluation is not to prove that a specific piece of training worked, it is to transform the whole learning process and significantly raise the probability of a training investment providing a good return. In order to fulfil this role, evaluation has to start at the diagnostic stage: there is not much point in carrying out a 'post-mortem'. Making the correct diagnosis at the beginning will give the patient the best chance of survival. Post-mortems can only be carried out after the patient has already expired.

So the initial question at the design stage now has to be: 'How will this training add value and how much value, in £s, will it produce?' This is a much more profound question than it might at first appear. The concept of added value implies much more than just a financial figure. Consider customer service training again. What would be the added value indicator at level 4 for a customer service programme? Would an improvement in customer satisfaction surveys or mystery shopper ratings satisfy level 4? They might appear to satisfy Kirkpatrick's ultimate level of 'results' but do they satisfy the added value criterion of £s? Until they do, they do not guarantee any beneficial, 'organisational' impact; either in theory or practice. Satisfied customers do not guarantee profitability. They may love the service but decide that it comes at a price they are not prepared to pay.

Furthermore, any search for subjective measures of 'intangibles' or qualitative data on customer satisfaction (eg customer reactions, brand loyalty) still has to take into consideration that there will only be a return on investment (ROI) if customer satisfaction eventually feeds through to sales. Only hard sales figures will provide the highest levels of confidence that the training is effective. But even that is not the end of the value chain. Increased sales volumes could have been achieved at heavy price discounts. So heavy, in fact, that profits on sales have actually fallen (eg a 5 per cent increase in sales of meals is only achieved after giving away a 10 per cent price reduction) and the result is a drop in organisational value.

So added value is not just sales figures, it is the net, residual value. It is the distillation of what is left after all the cost and effort has been expended in the search for business success. The most important insight that added value provides though, is that value does not come from just one part of the organisation; it is only produced when the whole organisation is working together effectively. Better table service from waitresses will add no value if the purchasing team buy sub-standard foodstuffs or the new chef produces inferior quality meals and drives customers away. This is why added value is the only, *ultimate* gauge of organisational impact or results. This is a much clearer definition of what level 4 has to mean. Added value is what can be banked after all other organisational issues and variables have been taken into account. It is the final analysis. It is the last word in evaluation.

SO HOW DO YOU GET ADDED VALUE?

Any attempt to add value, however, has to pass through an organisational, distillation process that consists of a very limited number of pipes. Value, in £s, can only come through one or a combination of these:

- reduced operational costs
- increased output or
- increased revenue.

To many seasoned businesspeople, never mind trainers, this will appear to be a ridiculously short list. What about 'creativity', 'innovation' and 'morale'? Why are they not on this list, you might ask. They are not on the list because none of them will automatically guarantee added value. Employees may have creative ideas for cost reduction, to raise production levels or even generate revenue but creativity, for the sake of it, is worthless. 'Being creative' is a meaningless statement unless and until it is converted into real value. Also, the ultimate arbiter of whether 'creativity' adds any value or not is the customer and whether they are prepared to pay for it.

Let us posit, for example, that as a direct result of attending a creativity training programme a waitress might think she is being creative by jumping onto a table to deliver a rendition of her favourite song. How would such unexpected behaviour be regarded by the customers or the management?

Is it likely to bring in more customers or frighten some of them off? If it results in lost custom then such creativity is sapping value from the organisation. It also seems rather perverse, from a business planning perspective, to produce such creative 'results' before you have done any market research to check whether customers would appreciate singing waitresses. Trying to offer new ideas to customers without testing them first could result in a total misalignment between business strategy and learning strategy.

Added value, level 4, evaluation, as a discipline in its own right, ensures such misalignment will never happen. This is because it forces all stakeholders to articulate what they expect the outcomes of training to be before the training starts, during the design phase. Training without a clear and pre-defined purpose or result in mind is, at best, serendipitous and, at worst, breaks all the fundamental rules of learning.

Some trainers may argue that they should not be held accountable if their best efforts do not add value. After all, it might not be their fault if the ultimate result is not added value, in extra £s. This could be true but added value is a very unforgiving master. It does not matter whose fault it is, apportioning blame does not, of itself, add any value. For this reason it is rather pointless to try to make any distinction between evaluating at the team, departmental or organisational levels (see Hamblin's Model in Appendix 2). Added value always measures the output from the complete process chain and everyone in it. It is systemic in the sense that it reveals that the whole system is working properly. The system produces value to the customer. So let us now look at a systemic evaluation model that is founded on this definition of value.

2 ■ DEALING WITH THE PRACTICALITIES

4 ■ THE BASELINE, ADDED VALUE, EVALUATION AND LEARNING SYSTEM

We need to remember that Kirkpatrick originally produced his model in 1959, at a time when training meant predominantly classroom based, tutor-led *courses* to trainees who had relatively simple needs. The pace of change was slower and questions about the real value of training were few and far between. We now live in a much more dynamic, pressurised, computerised, business environment; with far more sophisticated management information systems. In effect, Kirkpatrick gave us an abacus for evaluation when only simple calculations were required. What we need now is a much more versatile 'measurement technology' to cope with a greater variety of learning interventions. This will consist of a combination of a model, a system and some tools and techniques. So let us first establish the correct model.

Actually the model we are going to use looks almost identical to Kirkpatrick, but looks can be deceptive. Probably one of the biggest, yet most subtle, misunderstandings about Kirkpatrick's Model is that it is an 'evaluation' model. It should be and it could be but in practice it isn't. Let us consider evaluating a leadership programme and imagine that pre- and post-test scores reveal that one of the leadership trainees has learned something about the role of emotional intelligence in leadership. Let us go even further and suggest that someone assesses their emotional intelligence back in the workplace (that's at level 3) by getting feedback from their team. This shows that their colleagues believe their newly developed leader exhibits much greater emotional intelligence. So does this mean we have 'evaluated' his development? No. Only level 4 will answer the specific questions: 'What impact has this new emotional intelligence had on the organisation? What value has it added?' So let us look at a model that really focuses on providing a very convincing answer to this level 4 question.

THE BASELINE, ADDED VALUE, EVALUATION AND LEARNING MODEL

This model (in Figure 4.1) is meant to combine the first law of evaluation – pre-measurement – with a sound and robust theory of learning that says people only learn when they have feedback on their performance. However, it has only one critical step: the first step – Step 1. All the other steps (2–5) are optional.

Step 1 Baseline – pre-training

a   Establish how the proposed training is going to add value to the organisation.

b   Obtain performance measures for each trainee before the training starts.

Figure 4.1   The only way to the top level is to start at the baseline

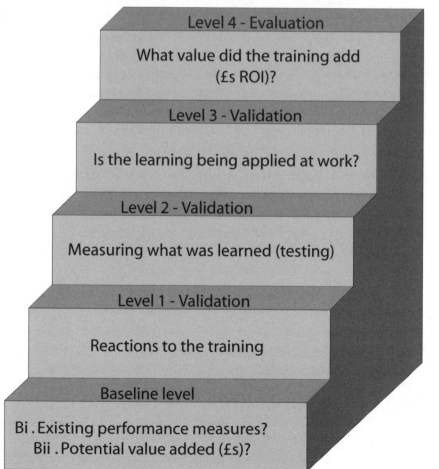

Level 4 - Evaluation

What value did the training add (£s ROI)?

Level 3 - Validation

Is the learning being applied at work?

Level 2 - Validation

Measuring what was learned (testing)

Level 1 - Validation

Reactions to the training

Baseline level

Bi . Existing performance measures?
Bii . Potential value added (£s)?

Steps 2 to 5 – post-training

2   Check reactions.

3   Check learning.

4   Check transfer/application.

5   Re-measure the performance of each trainee and calculate ROI (if appropriate).

If we apply this immediately to a simple sales training example we would have to ask the following baseline questions:

- How well is each salesperson currently performing (ie selling)? (say £1m).

- How much better might they perform (sell) if we train them? (say 2 per cent).

- What would this expected increase be worth in terms of sales revenue? (£1m × 2 per cent = £20,000).

- More importantly, how much more profit will that generate? (£20,000 × 10 per cent profit margin = £2000)

Hopefully this illustrates very clearly the difference between an evaluation model and one that just validates training. It is easy to demonstrate this with a sales example but a really good model should be able to cope with any learning intervention you might want to evaluate.

How about an e-learning project or a corporate university? Can the same principles, rules and questions apply at the baseline stage in the process? It appears that this immediately presents you with a practical problem: what measures of performance and value can you use?

Interestingly, when trainers who are new to the subject of evaluation reach this difficult point they assume that a different set of rules must apply. Or they conclude that there must be another way to measure or evaluate (some even try approaches such as Appreciative Enquiry – see Appendix 2). They find it difficult to accept that the rules of evaluation are simple, obvious, universally applicable and sacrosanct.

What they do not seem to understand is that no one invented the rules of evaluation. I certainly do not make up the rules any more than I could make up the economic laws of supply and demand. If you want to evaluate a piece of training then, in theory, there is no other way than following these steps. But I should also point out that using the Baseline Model is not as difficult or as onerous as you might think. In fact, most trainers who come across the Baseline Model for the first time are surprised to find that using it is easier and simpler than any other evaluation approach. It certainly will not result in the usual burden of laborious paperwork or questionnaires. You will only truly appreciate this point, however, when you actually put the Baseline Model into practice for yourself. Here is a quote from a very recent client, a training manager, who started to use the model for the first time:

> **❝** The biggest barrier for us so far is our 'customers' (not surprisingly) …. They are used to the 'old' way of doing things and do not like the discomfort of trying to tie training events to business objectives (as in some cases they are not even able to clearly describe their business objectives not to mention the skills necessary to achieve them). **❞**

Note how his line managers are struggling to 'describe their business objectives'. This is not uncommon and is the root cause behind the vast majority of evaluation problems. In fact, if the interface between the trainer and the line manager is not working very well the training will not work very well. This is why just having an evaluation model, on its own, is not enough. You, your line managers and everyone else in the organisation, have to work much more closely together. What you need to really make evaluation work is an evaluation system.

USING SYSTEMS

Mature organisations have mature, intelligent systems. Consider for a moment what this might actually look like in practice. Are you aware just how important systems are in organisations? Let us look at what a system does and then apply this to evaluation and learning.

> A system is a means for making happen what you want to happen.

The best systems are simple and must make sense. They should also be easily understood by everyone and influence their behaviour. Take, as an example, a traffic light system. We want to ensure that traffic starts and stops in a sequence. What we want to happen is a smooth flow of traffic. We also want no accidents to happen. Everyone would have to agree that this makes sense.

On paper, traffic lights are probably the nearest you will ever get to an example of a perfect system. However, there is more to traffic light systems than meets the eye. When you approach a traffic light and it turns from green to amber you have to make a decision whether to carry on through or stop. In that instant quite a few considerations flash through your mind. Will you be breaking the law? Will you cause an accident? Are you being irresponsible by not stopping? So systems in society inevitably become bound up with the values of society. We all believe it is morally right to obey the traffic light. Or, at least, the vast majority of us do.

However, the reason there is no such thing as a perfect system is that human beings will still make up their own mind whether to stick to the system or not. The best systems are those that are voluntarily accepted by everyone: everyone agrees on the rules and follows them. Unfortunately, some people will always be irresponsible and try to jump the lights. Usually they will get away with this but their selfish behaviour still threatens to undermine the whole system. If everyone ignored the lights, chaos would reign. That is why the rule of law exists, to provide a rock-solid foundation and deter transgressors.

Now let us transfer this idea of systems and behaviour to an organisational setting. The same principles apply. Organisational systems and personal values are interwoven. For example, we often hear references to command and control cultures when we are describing the way organisations operate. In such cultures the management impose control systems. You cannot spend any money unless you go through the budget system. Or you cannot choose another external supplier unless you follow the approval system. This type of system usually achieves the desired end – control – but in the process something is completely ignored: the intelligence, initiative and contribution of the individual.

Just to stretch the traffic light analogy as far as it will go: you might think that a perfect system would actually, physically, prevent anyone breaking the law. Traffic lights could have been designed in conjunction with a set of metal barriers that spring up out of the road physically to prevent anyone jumping the lights. However, this could easily create more problems. What if a driver did not notice that the lights were changing? They are likely to crash into the barriers; thereby defeating one of the objectives of traffic lights, which is to avoid accidents.

Enforcement of systems, therefore, might not be the best way forward. So what about trying the other extreme? On many junctions there are no lights, just a series of white lines. This is still a system but it relies much more heavily on the intelligence and attitude of the individual. Even further down the extreme end of this scale of allowing individuals to make up their own minds is the traffic regime in the Dutch province of Friesland, where they are experimenting with having no traffic signals or markings at all (www.homezonenews.org.uk/pdf/No4p4.pdf) and let drivers and pedestrians decide for themselves.

Every organisation has to decide for itself how it balances control systems with allowing employees freedom to act based on their intelligence and judgment. For example, how many times do managers want to act outside the company's control systems? They might want to use a new supplier but cannot, because the system demands that any new suppliers must have a given turnover to qualify. Nevertheless, the manager wants to take a risk on this new supplier, but the system is designed to avoid risk. Such systems can then seem to be preventing the manager running his or her department the best way they can. In such circumstances managers could reach the conclusion that the system does not make sense and feel they are involuntarily trapped by controls they do not support. This type of system produces many disadvantageous side-effects without the potential advantages that effective systems can bring. Maybe that new supplier could bring a significant cost saving.

Badly designed systems crush individuality and with it creativity, innovation and any chance of getting the best value out of people who really want to contribute. So what does the manager do? If they get too frustrated they might leave or they do their best to subvert the system. In effect they metaphorically try to jump the lights, but this is not an ideal solution. Now the behaviour of the individual manager could be working against the organisation: they help the new supplier to slip through the new supplier approval net but the new supplier goes bust, causing many more operational problems.

Probably the best solution is to aim to strike a balance between managing risk and maximising effectiveness. We really want the best of both worlds: brilliant systems that encourage the best behaviours which, in turn, lead to superb organisational performance. This brings us back to our main subject here, introducing an evaluation and learning system that is designed to do just that.

THE EVALUATION AND LEARNING SYSTEM

In order to produce such a system we need first to re-visit the training cycle (see Chapter 2) just one more time. In Figure 4.2 the Neo-Classical Cycle is now transformed into the Evaluation and Learning System. As with any system it is designed to make learning happen in order to improve organisational effectiveness. One thing you will notice though about this cycle is that it now has eight distinct phases. These may look very similar to the other cycles but we need to look at each one in more detail to understand fully exactly what is required of the trainer.

Phase 1 (Start) – Evaluate business needs

The longest, most critical and usually the most difficult phase. The question here though is quite simple. What does your business need: more revenue, lower costs, more productivity, greater margins or what? If you work for a public sector or not-for-profit

Figure 4.2 The Evaluation and Learning System

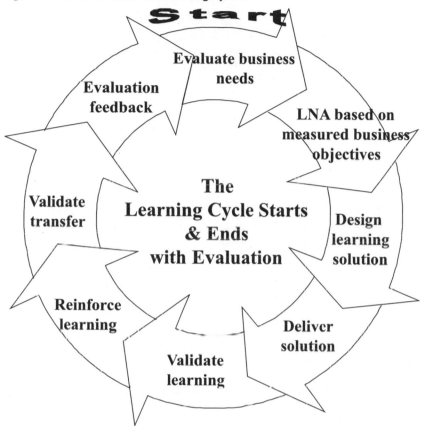

organisation the question is the same except you might substitute the term 'funding' for revenue. One thing that can be said about all business needs though is that they always have a £ sign attached. After all, everything comes at a cost.

If you want to talk about a business need in terms of 'market share', 'greater innovation' or 'time to market' this first phase demands that these needs be translated into hard figures so that everyone has the same appreciation of the importance and relative priority of these objectives. So, a one- point increase in market share from 5 per cent to 6 per cent (a 20 per cent increase in real terms) with existing sales of £10m will be equivalent to an extra £2m in sales (assuming the total market does not increase).

If we look at 'greater innovation', as a business need or objective, it will have to mean, ultimately, an increase in new product sales. There is no point in being innovative if customers do not buy your new product. Alternatively, innovation could produce a 10 per cent productivity improvement. If total direct costs are £7m, this 10 per cent saving will add up to £700k on the bottom line.

The simple rule here is that you cannot move on to phase 2 until the business need has been quantified and prioritised. If you do not follow this rule and, as a direct consequence, fail to pin down the underlying business need, it will inevitably result in the cycle starting from the wrong point. Any subsequent training will not then be directly linked to the business.

You should note here that we are now talking about a learning needs analysis or LNA, not a TNA. An LNA looks at all organisational issues, not just training.

Phase 2 – Learning needs analysis (LNA) based on measured business objectives

Following the market share example above, the marketing director has to be asked, right at the beginning of the business planning cycle, whether they will achieve the planned, one-point, increase in market share? If the answer they give is a straight and confident 'Yes' then a TNA might take this at face value and assume there are no training needs. However, an LNA will be a much more in-depth analysis. How is the marketing director going to achieve this increase: new products, a marketing campaign, better advertising or what?

Only when the marketing director shows some real concern is there an opportunity to drill down into possible learning needs. How about a poor track record of bringing new products to market on time and to the right quality? What has the organisation learned since the last new product launch?

You will already have noticed that this line of questioning takes considerably more time than simply asking 'What training do you need?' and is rarely going to result in a generic training solution. It is a process for tailoring specific learning solutions to specific individual, business-related needs. The links will be clear and closely connected. Even just asking these questions will improve the way your organisation learns and simultaneously increase the probability of a business payback. Bespoke learning will always prove to be a better investment than sheep-dip training

Phase 3 – Design learning solution

Regardless of how many questions are asked during phase 2 in this marketing example they might lead to an analysis of the product launch process. Who owns and has overall responsibility for this process? Why did the last launch not work so well? What was the business impact in terms of costs and delayed revenue streams?

No doubt an operational manager could lead a discussion on process analysis, but only if they had the skills and knowledge to do so. So we are inevitably back to analysing skills and knowledge gaps, but now it is within the context of a serious organisational issue, which already has some business measures, and £ signs attached.

Phase 4 – Deliver solution

The shortest and simplest phase of the entire cycle is usually phase 4. Having agreed on the measurable outcomes (eg cycle time improvements, launch cost reductions) the delivery phase will entail assembling the product launch process team and facilitating its development towards these agreed ends.

Phase 5 – Validate learning

During and after the process team meeting someone needs to check that people are actually learning what they need to know. The best person to do this should be the process expert called in to deliver the training. They will check that everyone fully understands the process, its boundaries and business impact.

Phase 6 – Reinforce learning

Any psychologist or learning expert will tell you all about the importance of the concept of reinforcement, so this extra phase is a conscious attempt to reinforce and embed what has been learned. Reinforcement in any learning cycle, however, should never be the responsibility of the trainer. They should ensure, right from phase 1, that the owner of the process and/or the business sponsor behind the learning activity should be the reinforcer. It is also their responsibility to check that everyone has been involved in redesigning the process so that it gains maximum buy-in from those who have to make it work. Moreover, if they find that any key personnel were excluded from the original team (eg product designers) they now have to bring them into the 'loop'.

It is worth pointing out here that this cycle is intended to act as a practical template. The business sponsor has to understand exactly what is required at each phase, in advance. The expectations of everyone involved have to be managed as well.

Phase 7 – Validate transfer

One of the biggest disappointments for any trainer is to see a potentially great piece of training fall at the final hurdle: where the learning is meant to transfer to the workplace. This phase is designed to check application because there are many organisational issues that can thwart the best-laid training plans.

We need to ask whether any new obstacles have been put in the way of successful transfer. Perhaps a senior manager pulls rank and says there are to be no changes in the product launch process? Maybe the product marketing team are at the mercy of late information from the technical team who were not involved in the process meetings?

It is unrealistic to say that all this should have been anticipated at the beginning. This is a learning system, after all, so it should expect to pick up new information and knowledge as it progresses. The whole purpose of phase 7 is an extra check that the cycle really is working and, if not, to pinpoint where it is breaking down.

Phase 8 – Evaluation feedback

Phase 8, feeding back what the evaluation is revealing, closes the loop on each turn of the cycle. This will not present the trainer with any problems if the whole cycle is designed with this end in mind. In this case, for example, choosing, during phase 1, to use sales figures one month after launch as the main criterion for success, will close the loop when these figures are available.

It would be disappointing if the target sales figure was not achieved but the whole purpose of evaluation in the learning cycle is to learn from the experience, regardless of the actual results. This then sets up the start of another turn of the cycle to make marketing even more effective. This is a continuous improvement, loop system.

The next big question though is what is all this effort really worth? Does it represent a good return on the initial investment and, if so, when do we get the payback? Only ROI will deliver the answer for us.

5 ■ ROI – WHAT IT CAN AND CANNOT DO

You should be able to discern from the title of this chapter that experience has taught me to have a very ambivalent attitude to ROI. ROI is a much abused and mis-used formula. The key to ROI is knowing its weaknesses as well as its strengths; its capabilities and limitations; how to use it; when to use it and when not to use it. On one level it will never be more than just a simple, financial calculation, but it can be adapted and interpreted in different ways, to great effect. Unfortunately, though, as with most other aspects of evaluation, perceptions, human behaviour and historical baggage all have a part to play.

The search for ROI seems to have become the new Holy Grail for many training departments, but usually for all the wrong reasons. It is often used to try and *prove* the benefits of training, in order to *justify* training spend and thereby ensure the continued existence of the training department. These aims are usually symptomatic of training departments in trouble, rather than those doing everything they can to add value to the organisation through learning. However, before we look at the best way to use ROI let us be clear what the formula is and how to produce the necessary figures.

THE ROI FORMULA

It is worth noting that at this stage we are only covering the main principles behind the formula and will not consider how to produce the actual figures until later.

The formula shown in Figure 5.1 is made up of seven pieces of information:

a   *Gross benefit achieved from training* – if sales improve by £1 million and the profit on these extra sales is 10 per cent then a figure of £100,000 would be inserted.

b   *Cost of training (or investment) (above the line)* – simply all the costs associated with the initial analysis, design, development and delivery of the training

Figure 5.1   Calculating returns using the ROI formula

Net ROI $= \dfrac{\text{Gross Benefit from training (£)} - \text{Cost of training (£)}}{\text{Cost of training (£)}} \times 100$ per cent

Which can reduced to –

Net ROI $= \dfrac{\text{Net Benefit from training(£)}}{\text{Cost of training (£)}} \times 100$ per cent

And if we insert some numbers –

Net ROI $= \dfrac{£100,000 - £50,000}{£50,000} \times 100$ per cent

Net ROI $= \dfrac{£50,000}{£50,000} = 1 \times 100$ per cent

Net ROI is therefore 100 per cent per annum.

However, if we assume that the same benefits accrue each year for another two years then the ROI is 500 per cent over three years (ie (£300,000 - £50,000) divided by £50,000).

programme – let us assume this is £50,000. This has to be deducted from the gross benefit (a, above) leaving the net benefit (see next paragraph).

c   *The net benefit achieved from training* – in this case the net or residual benefit is therefore £50,000.

d   *Cost of training (below the line)* – although this is the same figure as b, it is used below the line so that the net benefit can be shown as a return on the original training cost or investment.

e   *Net ROI* – the monetary return on the original investment after the cost of the training is paid back or recouped.

f   *✕ 100 per cent* – this converts the Net ROI monetary amount into a percentage return on the original investment.

g   *per annum – payback period in years* – this is not actually shown in most ROI calculations. There is usually an assumption that the benefit will be accrued in one year. If, however, you wish to assume that the same benefits continue to accrue in future years (ie the salespeople continue to sell at the higher level without any further training costs) then the number of years should be factored in by multiplying a by the number of years chosen. In the example given this would produce a net return of 500 per cent over three years based on a reasonable assumption that the salespeople will stay with the company for at least another two years on average.

Once you have all the necessary information required by the formula the calculation itself is can very easily be completed using a calculator. After a bit of practice, however, it is quick and easy to calculate the percentage return using simple mental arithmetic.

However, one can easily understand why many trainers do not recognise the importance of the ROI calculation. They do not wish to see their professionalism, creativity and innovative practices reduced to such a rigid, simple formula; especially one invented by and for accountants. Moreover, they believe that such a cold calculation cannot capture all the equally important, but incidental, soft and intangible benefits that they believe occur as a result of training.

This sort of thinking, of course, is based on a complete misunderstanding of what ROI can do for the learning process. As with evaluation, measuring ROI is not the only benefit to be gained from using this formula. Discussing potential ROI should actually be used as a positive and constructive element of training analysis and design. Even at a conceptual level ROI can be incredibly powerful. It crystallises, perfectly, what the purpose of any training or development initiative is. It might look as if it will turn training into a simplistic, black-and-white exercise but this is certainly not the case in practice (although see Appendix 2 for comments about the Jack Phillips approach and the 'American obsession' with trying actually to measure ROI).

MEASURING ROI

Despite my own interest in ROI as a discipline, as suggested above, the growing interest in the subject is being driven by training departments which are desperately trying to justify their existence. This is a very negative and defensive way of employing ROI. It is also usually a rather futile, self-defeating exercise because the results are often unconvincing and fail to show a direct, causal connection between training and business performance. Moreover, while ROI is always relatively easy to calculate for sales training, it really comes into its own, paradoxically, when the benefits are not so easy to calculate.

To explain what I mean, and without wishing to become too pedantic, it is very important to view the whole subject of training ROI from three different perspectives. We can talk about:

- ROI the concept
- ROI the practical formula or
- ROI the management tool.

So what are the differences?

ROI – THE CONCEPT

In Chapter 2 it was suggested that the purpose of all organisational training is to produce some benefit for the organisation. That benefit should either be the generation of basic value (see page **45**) or added value. Added value can only be gauged in terms of either an increase in revenue or a saving through reduced operational costs. Added value always has a £ sign and ROI is the means for calculating how large that £ sign is over a given period.

Anyone should be able to understand the *concept* of ROI, even if they do not bother to measure physically the extra £s generated. So why is it so important even at just a conceptual level? Because the concept or notion of getting a return on training investment will dictate both training and development strategy and policies. If the board fully understands and subscribes to the concept of ROI they will not endorse any training that is not intended to provide a bottom line, organisational benefit with a clear payback.

Of course, if you are a training director, you could eschew the whole concept of ROI and produce a policy that says individual development is an end in itself and worthy of receiving company resources and support. Some employee development and assistance programme are predicated on this basis. The only problem with this policy is it is either completely open-ended, which means you have no way of prioritising or selecting where you spend the money, or you impose a totally arbitrary figure on how much each employee can have. This policy appears to be based on no inherent logic or sense of allocating resources according to real need, and as such stands on very shaky foundations.

The concept of ROI, on the other hand, provides a much firmer footing for a learning strategy. Learning has to be fully aligned with what the organisation needs to know and ROI ensures all training and development is directly aligned with business needs. Assuming this, in itself, is a strong enough argument for you to adopt the concept of ROI, we can now move on to consider the practical implications.

ROI – THE PRACTICAL FORMULA

Talking about ROI at a conceptual level is relatively easy but it is another thing entirely actually to carry it out in practice. Figure 5.2 shows the ROI formula using a real example taken from a customer service training programme in a retail business. Now, if we look at each step in the process of producing these figures some of the findings are quite alarming.

Figure 5.2 Applying ROI to customer service training

$$\text{Net ROI} = \frac{\text{Gross Benefit from training (£)} - \text{Cost of training (£)}}{\text{Cost of training (£)}} \times 100 \text{ per cent}$$

$$\text{Eg Net ROI} = \frac{£3.7M - £1.4M}{£1.4M} \times 100 \text{ per cent}$$

$$= 165 \text{ per cent}$$

Here is a brief background to this piece of training. The programme itself was very short, literally just a few hours, and was delivered by tutors to groups of up to 15 people at a time. The programme was being rolled out to 15,000 employees and the company was already nine months into an 18-month roll-out when I was asked to help them produce an ROI figure for the programme.

The cost (or investment)

The easiest task, from a practical perspective, was to work out the cost of the training. Many of the costs were obvious (ie course costs, tutor fees, materials, venue and catering) and notional amounts were included for office space, development costs and anything else that was legitimately regarded as part of the equation.

When calculating costs yourself it is advisable to take every possible cost into account although the figures do not have to be perfectly accurate (unless you have a finance director who demands this). If you anticipate that somebody might want to dispute the costs figures you produce then add on 50 per cent as your margin for error. Always over-estimate the costs. After all, it is not the cost that is of primary importance in an ROI calculation, it is the benefit. Any business leader will be more interested in the return on the investment, rather than the cost in isolation. In this example the training team had already calculated the costs at £1.4 million.

The benefit (in £s)

Trying to put a £ sign on the benefits of training is the problematic piece in this jigsaw. But then so is calculating the benefits of an advertising campaign or even the rental income from a new office block. All business is about speculation and the risk of the unknown. The trick here is not to try and work to a higher standard of credibility than anyone else in the organisation. If accountants are prepared to guess at amortisation costs or marketing directors to guess about market share why should a trainer not be prepared to have a guess at the potential benefits from training?

One 'rule of thumb' assumption or estimate that I recommend when using ROI is that any training should improve the performance of the trainees by at least 1 per cent. If the focus of the training is sales then this figure is 1 per cent of profit on sales. If the focus is reducing operating costs then show a 1 per cent cost saving. If you are struggling to find any figures then assume a 1 per cent salary saving by improving employee productivity (ie if 100 employees improve their productivity by 1 per cent then you can now afford to lose one of them with no loss in overall productivity).

However, this is where we start to cross the line between theory and practice, from concept to actual result. In the example shown above the benefit figure of £3.7 million was an assumed 1 per cent increase in profit from sales as a direct result of improved customer service. Now, once the actual figures are estimated something quite remarkable happens – vague notions of training become crystallised, spontaneously. For example, store managers can now be told that their sales should go up by at least this amount as a direct result of the training. This then starts to transform the whole training and learning process. It starts to change management behaviour and produces a very different modus operandi for training.

ROI – THE MANAGEMENT TOOL

You may never have considered this before but all training and development is based on a hypothesis. If we train person A to do activity B (listen to customer needs) it should result in C (more sales). Yet no trainer has magic powers and their hypotheses could be completely wrong but no one will ever know unless we check the training afterwards. All we can do in advance is speculate and hope for the best.

In this particular case one would assume that the hypothesis behind the customer service programme was that the training would improve customer service and satisfaction, thereby increasing customer retention and the extra referrals and recommendations that would inevitably follow. All of this would then lead, in turn, to higher sales and profits. This all sounds very obvious until you discover that the hypothesis behind this particular programme was far from clear.

Checking the thinking behind a training programme is one of the most powerful ways in which to use ROI as a management tool. It immediately and very simply checks that the hypothesis behind the training is valid and sound. So, in this case, I first checked with the retail training team that the real objective behind seeking to improve customer service was actually an attempt to increase sales. They were unsure what the real objective was but accepted that ultimately it must be sales if it was to be worth anything at all. Yet, when I then looked at the actual content of the programme I found that there was a clear statement to the trainees that this was not designed as a sales training course!

So the ROI questions had already unearthed some serious problems with this programme. Nevertheless, we applied the 1 per cent rule to produce the numbers in Figure 5.2. Their annual profit on sales was £370 million so 1 per cent equated to £3.7 million, producing a return of 165 per cent. In other words, even a poorly designed training programme, as long as it hit the mark 1 per cent of the time, would still produce a very healthy return. There is only one problem with this reverse engineering approach though: no one believes the figures it produces.

This leads us back to the fundamental problem: the level of ignorance about evaluation in many training departments. Trainers who think evaluation and ROI should only be done *after* the training has finished usually have to reverse engineer or 'retro fit' the results to the training. This is completely the wrong way round. Searching for a post-training ROI inevitably makes the training team look inept rather than helping them to improve their results and credibility.

So let us try to wind back the clock here and consider how ROI could have really transformed this particular, perceived, customer satisfaction issue.

ROI ALARM BELLS

When first contacted by a prospective client to undertake ROI work there is a series of questions that I normally ask.

1   What are the business objectives behind the training?

2   When will it take place?

3   Who is asking questions about ROI?

4   Why do they want to know the ROI?

5   What will you do with the results?

To anyone with ROI expertise any wrong answers will immediately set off an alarm bell in their head. So what sort of answers are 'wrong'?

1   In this case the objective was 'customer service', not sales. This made me realise the training team did not realise there was a difference.

2   It had already been running for nine months. ROI should always be designed-in, before the training starts.

3　The person asking the ROI questions was the commercial director, not the training team. Ironically, it was the commercial director who bought in this particular training in the first place. He purchased the programme from the ex-CEO of another retail business. Yet the two retail businesses had absolutely nothing in common.

4　The reason they wanted to know the ROI nine months into the programme was because, even though they had not explicitly stated that they wanted the programme to generate sales, they could see no general sales improvement and wanted to know why.

5　Unfortunately, any evaluation would now only demonstrate just how ill-conceived the training programme had been, right from the start. This would have made everyone involved look inept. So would they really want to see the results and would they all learn something from this exercise?

In this particular case there were quite a few alarm bells, all ringing at once. So how can you ensure this never happens to you?

What I like about the concept of ROI in training, a notoriously nebulous area of management, is that it is so definite. It is the clearest statement one could ever make about the purpose behind training. It states that as long as the benefit is greater than the cost then the training is worthwhile.

However, many trainers try to pretend that training is not this straightforward. A delegate on a workshop I once ran on the subject of ROI asked, 'Can I put "increased employee morale" under the "benefit" part of the equation?' The answer to which is 'No', unless you can show a clear connection between improved morale and cost savings or revenue improvements. But this is where the debate really starts to heat up.

AGREEING AN ROI OBJECTIVE INFLUENCES TRAINING DESIGN

Having argued so far in support of the concept of ROI you might find it hard to believe that I do not actively promote measuring ROI in training, except in very special circumstances. This may sound hypocritical so perhaps I should explain.

My earlier book on evaluation (*Maximising your ROI in Training* (2000)) goes to great lengths to explain the use of measurement principles when undertaking training needs analysis and designing effective learning solutions. What it does not do though is produce masses of data or metrics. This is a point commonly misunderstood by trainers who just assume evaluation means measuring everything to the nth degree.

Once the training team in the retail example above accepted that 'better customer satisfaction' meant more sales revenue the whole thrust of the programme changed:

- The reference to it *not* being a sales training programme was removed

- Now we could ask the specific question 'How much more revenue do we want?'

- This leads to the question – 'From which stores?'

- This in turn prioritises the training delivery to the stores that need the training most.

- It also means the relevant store managers have to buy-in to the revenue targets.

- That means they have to take a greater interest in the training.

- They also have to think about who gets trained.

- At the individual and team level the improvement targets should motivate and provide feedback.

- The generic piece of training now becomes an integrated and highly focused learning exercise.

Obviously, to obtain the correct level of commitment to this programme involves resolving many of the soft issues implicit, but hidden, within this initiative. Senior management ownership, store manager accountability, individual trainees who now have to accept that they have to help in 'selling' to the customer. ROI, perhaps surprisingly, brings many underlying organisational issues to the surface.

It is also worth reiterating that the discipline of ROI is not the sole preserve of trainers in the commercial sector. It can play an equally important role in the public and not-for-profit sectors. Below is an example taken from the world of international healthcare.

USING ROI AT THE WORLD HEALTH ORGANISATION

Those new to the discipline of ROI often think it is only suitable for highly commercialised organisations with clear profit and loss figures. I have to admit that it is certainly easier to use ROI in a sales-based operation but it can be used in any organisation, including not-for- profit. The results can be startling.

In 2002 I was asked by one of the regional operations of the World Health Organisation (WHO) to help them produce some ROI figures for health training programmes. This was an interesting angle on ROI because the benefits of health training should be quite obvious and significant. However, the WHO, like any other organisation, has many competing demands for limited funds so one of the issues they required clarification on was relative priorities.

Two particular areas for potential training spend were HIV/AIDS awareness and nosocomal or hospital acquired infections (ie additional infections picked up by patients while they are in hospital). So how do you fix priority between these two? Using ROI requires you to attach a benefit figure (in this case £s) to each, but where do we obtain these figures?

In the case of HIV/AIDS an official economic report put the cost of the spread of AIDS in the region concerned at £2 billion between 2000 and 2005. As always, the rule of thumb ROI proposition is initially based on an expected 1 per cent improvement. So if the whole of the WHO training budget (£600k) were spent just on HIV education and this resulted in a 1 per cent reduction in the incidence of aids (worth £20 million) then the ROI would be 3,233 per cent.

Similar figures were gathered on the incidence of nosocomal infections in the local hospital and the costs of dealing with them were used to do a comparison. Spending £5,000 on training someone in infection control, again assuming a 1 per cent improvement, produced a potential ROI of 0.8 per cent over the same period. Of course, the WHO would like to do both but with limited funds they have to make difficult choices. Using ROI helped to clarify their priorities and facilitate the decision-making process.

So, rather than confusing the issue, ROI should provide clarity of purpose, aid the evaluation process and assist with priorities. Now we will look at some more specific tools and techniques that will enable you to deal with many of the other issues associated with evaluation.

6 ■ EVALUATION TOOLS AND TECHNIQUES

Many trainers have become very wary of evaluation. It makes them accountable. They generally only do it when they have to and even then only at the lowest level possible (level 1 – happy sheets). Yet we now know that the most common trap to ensnare trainers is the fallacious belief that they can leave any considerations of evaluation until the training intervention is completed. Evaluation is impossible if clear measures have not already been *'built-in'* at the training design stage (see Chapter 4).

The most important principle of evaluation, therefore, is to have crystal clear objectives *before* any training is designed. So all the tools and techniques offered here are designed to help produce such objectives and then design measures *in* to the training for evaluation purposes.

TOOL 1. THE PROBABILITY CHECK

Purpose and use – to ensure training has a reasonable probability of being effective.

In Chapter 2 we looked at the theory of probability and asked what the chances were of a piece of training or development being effective. This can easily be used as a simple tool when deciding whether or not to do a particular piece of training.

First, you can assume, before any discussion takes place, that any piece of training will have a 50:50 chance of success (ie a probability of 1\2). This is not a very realistic assumption because it would mean that even the most off-the-wall events (eg firewalking) would have as much chance of success as a piece of well-conceived training. However, it does not matter too much because this tool will aim to increase or decrease this level of probability to a point where it helps you to make a clear-headed decision about spending money. Poorly designed programmes will not pass this test.

This tool uses all the principles of learning and evaluation covered throughout this book to gauge whether an intervention is worth making or not. Take a leadership programme as an example. You could assume that sending a group of managers to one of the main management colleges for a leadership programme starts with a 50:50 chance of success (ie 1\2). Then you can consider what factors will either increase (+s) or decrease (−s) this probability. Any training plan that ends up with more minuses than pluses should not be pursued. This simple plus/minus scoring system usually works well but if the final result is still not convincing then weighted scores can be used. That is, those factors with a potentially significant positive impact on probability could be given a score of ++ (eg every trainee has a personal performance objective linked to the training) while those with a potentially significant negative impact could be given − (eg a senior manager voices their lack of commitment).

In Tables 6.1 below the various scores are shown for 11 separate statements resulting in a net − score. This is a lower probability than required and the leadership programme idea needs to be either re-thought or discarded. If anything, weighting the scores in this particular case is likely to result in even lower probability (eg the lack of pre-measures could be worth another -).

▷ Table 6.1 Training and development effectiveness – probability check

Start with a score of ? – then add the score in brackets for a 'yes' and deduct for a 'no' on each of the following statements	Plus/minus scores
We have defined leadership clearly	−
Pre-measures have been taken	−
Every delegate has been fully briefed	+
Every delegate has agreed with the method of development	+
Every delegate has pre-determined objectives	−
We have a line-of-sight to real business needs	−
This is the best leadership programme we could find	−
We have followed the learning cycle	−
We have already arranged follow-up	+
All delegates have to report results back after 6 months	+
The board are fully aware and supportive of this programme	+
Net score	−

Some of the statements shown in this example could be applied to almost any training and development intervention, while others would be specifically tailored. For a customer service training programme, for example, there may be a statement saying 'Each delegate has been provided with the mystery shopper scores for their area'.

TOOL 2. THE INPUT/OUTCOME/OUTPUT TEST

Purpose and use – to ensure you measure the right things.

It is crucial in evaluation to measure the right things. This tool is short and simple but ensures that you concentrate any evaluation effort on the things that matter: outputs, not inputs or outcomes. So what's the difference? For example, the inputs that go into making beer are hops, barley, water and heat. The outcome is a barrel of beer. The output is the money the customer pays for a pint. Of course, without the inputs there would be no beer but inputs and outcomes do not guarantee the output you want, profit. If the beer is not sold the value of the output is zero.

Evaluators should always view training from this perspective. You might feel inclined to measure only inputs (eg the number of people who choose to attend a course) or even outcomes (eg the percentage who enjoyed it) in the belief that it will guarantee the right outputs. However, only output measures will provide the answer. So let us make a clear distinction between these three terms when applied to training.

Training inputs

time
effort
money (percentage of paybill spent on training)
coaching
training courses
e-learning content
e-learning number of site 'hits'
e-learning user sessions
competence modules
number of participants
number of training days

should lead to:

Training outcomes

skills
knowledge
changed behaviours

which should then lead to:

Training outputs

    cost reductions
    higher sales
    profit
    provision of more goods or services
    speedier development of new products or services
    improved quality of service.

Now to illustrate that this is not just a semantic distinction, a director of a large e-learning provider told me that they evaluated the benefits of the e-learning they provided for a government department by calculating that it saved them £6 million when compared to traditional classroom tuition. I advised him though that this was not an evaluation because the cost of the training was, and always would be, just an input figure. First, he could only claim a £6 million saving if the outcomes (skills and knowledge acquired) were at least equal to those delivered in the classroom.

But even that would not be a true evaluation. All of this training, whether delivered in a classroom or online, could be worthless if it was the wrong type of training. The only way to gauge whether it was good value training or not would be to measure how the government department was performing before and after the training. Its outputs (eg satisfied customers) would be the only way to evaluate the training.

Once you are clear about the difference you can move on to use the next tool which will tell you what is and isn't a valuable output.

TOOL 3. THE ADDED VALUE SCANNER

Purpose and use – to focus all training and development on value creation.

If you refer back to the model in Figure 4.2 in Chapter 4 (the learning system) the first step is to 'evaluate business needs'. Another way of putting this is to ask the question 'Where are the biggest opportunities for creating value?' Of course, all other directors in the business should be asking this same question and coming up with ideas that their function can deliver. So marketing is looking for untapped markets, the sales director is seeking new sales opportunities, operations want to find cost savings and new technology, R&D are trying to discover the next new blockbuster product. So, anyone heading up a training and development function should also have one eye on how training can add value. This tool not only aims to identify an opportunity for value creation but one that can only be exploited as a result of some training.

The best way to use this piece of equipment is to imagine looking through the type of x-ray, scanning machine used at airports. These scanners remove all surface layers to reveal the contents underneath. The added value scanner similarly strips away anything that gets in the way of revealing the value underneath. Often the search for value is confused (eg let's improve creativity) and distracted by the 'white noise' produced by culture (eg we can't take that risk) and any internal politics (eg no one is prepared to accept responsibility). So visualise, if you can, putting your organisation through this x-ray scanner.

What this scanning machine actually produces is a very detailed picture of the four key variables that drive any organisation; nothing else registers on the screen. These variables are:

Output – that is the number of goods or services you provide per annum (eg TVs manufactured, pints brewed, number of clients supported by a social services department).

Costs – the cost of providing those outputs.

Revenue – the income received, either from selling the outputs or from other funding sources (government funding, charitable donations).

Quality – the outputs produced without defects or requiring reworking, the level of customer satisfaction achieved.

The scan itself involves looking at the organisation's strategy, business plan and operating plan purely through these four variables and asking the simple question: where are we now on each of these? How much do we produce, how high are our costs, what levels of income are we achieving and what sort of quality standard do we have? But note, these are all *measurement* questions – you are looking for existing measures. Why? Because the Baseline Evaluation Model demands it. These measures will be your baseline for evaluation. They will also enable you to calculate potential ROI quickly (see Chapter 5).

Of course, if we look at just one of these variables, such as costs, then you will need to drill down until you find a specific measure attached to a specific individual (eg a production supervisor, a hospital ward manager or a shop manager is unable to meet his or her cost targets) Only then can you ask the question: will we be able to help this individual to achieve a cost saving through training and development?

However, the scanner is a much more powerful piece of equipment than you might imagine and has three settings. Moreover, you are strongly advised not to try switching it onto full power until you are totally competent and have developed a high degree of confidence.

Its first setting is a broad organisational scan as already described. On the second setting you can zoom in to focus on a specific training idea that is just at the discussion stage. For example, it could be something like a change management or customer service programme or even a new management competence model. Take the scanner along to the next project meeting and ask your colleagues whether they can see any added value variables lying underneath this programme.

This will receive a very mixed response initially. Some will suggest that there is more to added value than just these four variables. You will need to stand your ground though because there isn't. If they say the new programme is intended to increase innovation in the organisation then this should be covered by all four variables. In fact you have to be quite innovative to generate added value but the innovation is only worthwhile if you produce more goods and services and receive extra revenue as a result.

However, if no one can say how the training will add value you have a serious problem. This training, if it goes ahead, will not be working to the learning system outlined in Chapter 4 and will therefore have no commitment or reinforcement built in.

Let us assume for the moment though that the project team accept the basic principles of added value and suggest that the main variable for the change management programme is increased efficiency (ie possibly more output and at a lower cost). Now you can turn up the scanner to full power. You suggest that the project team needs to think through exactly what this would look like in practice. You may need to set a date for another meeting to do this but you should at least have a quick practice run straight away using the third and most powerful setting

On this setting the scanner is going to provide an individual, full body scan. To start this scan, personalise it. Imagine there is a real person going through it. Pick an actual, named individual — say an operations or production manager called Phil Brown — and consider how he will fare if he ends up on the change management programme? What does the team expect Phil to do as a result of attending this programme? If anyone says 'change his behaviour' ask them 'How?' Also, ask them why Phil should be willing to change his behaviour? What's in it for him? Then ask what exactly Phil can do to add value through lower costs.

As this discussion develops it will soon become apparent that:

- 'Change management' means a many different things to different people.

- Until everyone agrees what the objectives are it is unlikely that any change will happen.

- 'Change' without measurable improvement will be meaningless.

- Phil's motivation and commitment to change will be dependent on his motivation and commitment to achieve a cost reduction objective.

- Phil, in production, might not be able to reduce costs if the main determinant of operational costs is the materials required to build the product to the high specification contract agreed by the sales team with the customer.

- Consequently Phil and someone from the sales team will have to learn, together, how to reduce costs.

- This should influence the design of the programme.

By now you should start to realise just how powerful the scanner questions are. The ability to maintain a focus on value keeps training and development, and everyone involved in the value chain, focused on value throughout. Moreover, once you are proficient in using the scanner, at all three power settings, you will find it an invaluable piece of equipment in any learning intervention whether it be coaching, mentoring or e-learning.

One limitation of the scanner though is that it does not distinguish between the two types of value that we identified in Chapter 3: basic and added value. So it should be used in conjunction with another technique called the 3 Box System.

TOOL 4. THE 3 BOX SYSTEM

> Purpose and use – to prioritise training spend and to help to decide whether to evaluate or validate.

In Chapter 3 we identified the two types of organisational activity, those that produce 'basic value' and those that produce 'added value'. Now we are going to use this distinction or categorisation to form the foundation for another very simple but powerful tool: the 3 Box System. The three boxes in question are:

Box 1 – 'Must have' training – training that has to be done (ie learning that has to happen) to provide the basic value of the organisation.

Box 2 – Added value training – discretionary training but designed to produce added value with £ signs.

Box 3 – 'Nice to have' training – that is any other training that does not have such a clear purpose as in Boxes 1 and 2.

The system is designed to:

- Provide a simple framework for discussing training priorities with key sponsors and all other stakeholders in the training process, including trainees and their managers.

- Ensure that line management are fully committed to training and development.

- Enable the allocation of training budgets, on an agreed basis, for maximum returns.

- Select and apply the most appropriate validation and evaluation techniques for each type of training.

Any trainer or manager can immediately use the 3 Box System. All they have to do is make a list of existing training interventions and quickly decide which box each one falls into. As this system is designed to be an iterative process, though, it does not matter how accurate the first attempt is. Figure 6.1 below shows what types of training, typically, fall into which box, although there is no 'one-size-fits-all' solution here. Every piece of training has to be considered on its own merits and in its own particular context.

Figure 6.1 The 3 Box System

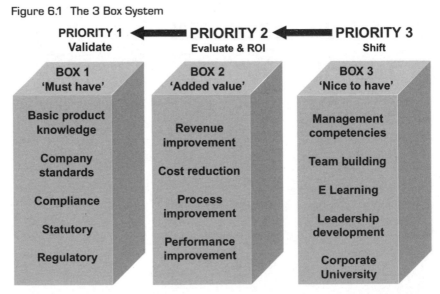

This system can be applied to any and every type of education, training, or development programme. However, its deceptively simple appearance belies a much more profound system. Like chess, it only takes a few minutes to learn the bare essentials but requires much longer to master.

So let us look at each box in more detail (but see also Chapter 3).

Box 1: Basic, 'must have' training

Basic or must have training is virtually self-explanatory. You cannot run your organisation without it. Your business may not fail immediately without it but over a period of time it will suffer. For example, you cannot sell your products if you have not trained your people in product knowledge. Equally, some training is done because the law or other external bodies demand it, such as health and safety training or that required for compliance purposes (eg exams have to be passed in the financial services sector).

But Box 1 is also closely related to the standards that your organisation sets for itself. A restaurant chain trains its waiting staff to know every ingredient of every item on its menu. That is the standard of customer service it has set for itself and so it has to have training that will deliver this standard.

Box 1 training needs are usually self-evident and obvious (eg new product features, technical training, how to operate equipment and systems) but because they could be described as merely helping the organisation to 'tread water' there is no sense of business improvement. Another way to look at basic training is that it gives the organisation no competitive advantage because your competitors will have to do the same sort of training. They also have to satisfy the same regulatory standards.

Box 2: Added value training

Added value is an entirely different proposition to basic training. While Box 1 training *must* be provided, there is no automatic mandate for Box 2 training. It is discretionary because the operation will not come to a halt without it. But if you choose to spend money in this Box it should give you an advantage over your competitors. If your sales people are trained 'better' than your competitors' then your sales should grow more than theirs. The improved profitability is the added value.

However, for any training activity to qualify for Box 2 you must have some understanding of *how* it will add value and how much value it will add in £££s. So training can only go in Box 2 after it has been through the scanner. Box 2 training should also be subjected to an ROI calculation that looks at expected benefits (in £££s) against the cost of the training. Only by doing so can it be given a priority relative to any other investment decisions.

ROI and the 3 Boxes

It is worth just pausing here for a moment to make some very important points about how to use ROI in conjunction with the 3 Box System.

First there is a general recommendation that you should not try to undertake an ROI for Box 1 training except in very exceptional circumstances (see also question 3 on 'control groups' in Appendix 1). Take the training of airline pilots for example. Teaching them how to take off and land would be Box 1, basic training: all airlines work to the same standard, the value of this training is obvious. However, maybe training in flying techniques that save fuel would fall into Box 2, the added value category, because we could calculate specific figures for fuel savings (eg fuel cost per flight) that we expect all pilots to achieve after being trained.

You may have noticed that in this particular case the basic pilot training is actually *critical* training. This might lead you to think that it must therefore have a high value, but every airline manages to achieve this standard so it has the same value for each of them. Of course, if you were trying to justify the cost of such training though you might try a control group experiment where you do not bother to train one of the new intake of trainee pilots, just to prove what the cost of not training is. This is not to be recommended though, for obvious reasons.

However, while ROI is not appropriate for Box 1 it is almost imperative in Box 2. Let us be absolutely clear what we are saying here though. This does not mean that all Box 2 training has to be mechanistically measured against strict ROI criteria. The main reason for *asking* the ROI question is still sound and worthwhile. It is the ROI question that checks whether there is any attempt to make a connection between a training intervention and a bottom line objective. It is this line-of-sight which is critical in any learning process if it is to remain focused. Moreover, carrying out nominal ROI calculations for a range of training activities helps to prioritise them in terms of their potential added value. In other words, is the potential value of a training programme worth £1 or £1,000,000?

For example, an HRD VP was asked how much of an ROI he achieved on the £50,000 per year that he spent on training administrative staff. When a 'hypothetical' ROI calculation was carried out the resulting ROI was negative. As a consequence of this he decided that he would have to either cease running this training altogether or at least revisit what it was meant to achieve.

Box 3 – 'Nice-to-have' training

Having now made the distinction between the two main categories or Boxes of training there is one further category: the 'nice to have' category, otherwise known as 'take-it-or-leave-it' training. The only training that comes under this heading is *that which failed to satisfy the criteria to get into Boxes 1 and 2*. That is, it is neither mandatory nor does it have a line of sight to a measurable improvement with a £ sign attached. No one should ever consciously design training to be in Box 3. Such training is the last priority and it is highly questionable whether it should happen at all. The probability of it adding any value to the organisation is very low.

Take the sort of event where a team spends a day away together to bond or develop team spirit. Whether such activity could be called 'training' is debatable but, regardless of what we call it, if it was not an absolute must and no one bothered to consider how it might add value, then it just falls into Box 3. It can only be categorised as 'nice to have' simply because everyone was quite happy to attend. Similarly, a corporate university without mandatory qualifications or measurable improvements go in Box 3. Management competence frameworks that allow managers to stay on without having achieved the desired level of competence fall into Box 3.

In my experience, where organisations fail to undertake effective training needs analysis, they can have over 50 per cent of their training budget in Box 3, primarily because they spend a lot of money on high cost initiatives (corporate universities, e-learning, etc) with no attempt to establish a potential ROI or to set tests to check that minimum standards have been met.

By the way, if you think you can cheat at the 3 Box 'game' by ignoring the rules, forget it. Putting training into Box 1 does not suddenly and miraculously make it a better investment. It is easy to spot when this is happening because no testing takes place to ensure that the training is meeting any standard. So even if you think you might be getting away with it your organisation isn't. A take-it-or-leave-it attitude to training is what consigns it to Box 3 and as it is unlikely to add any value it is the last priority. So, if you had to reduce your training budget by 10 per cent next year, Box 3 is the first place to make savings. Everything in Boxes 1 and 2 has a much clearer business justification.

Prioritising training budgets

With your new understanding of the 3 Boxes you can now identify where your current training budget goes simply by allocating costs to each training activity and then totalling the costs under each Box. When all costs have been allocated calculate what percentage of your budget is spent on each priority area. As a rule of thumb, it is likely that this will look something like 70 per cent (Box 1), 15 per cent (Box 2) and 15 per cent (Box 3) in an organisation with a systematic approach to training.

Box 1 typically takes up the biggest percentage, for many reasons, including the proliferation of new products, new legislation, new systems and the inevitability of employee turnover and the need for ongoing development.

If your own figures are similar to those suggested the first question to ask is why are you throwing away 15 per cent of your training budget on Box 3? No one takes Box 3 training seriously. It could, in theory, still be of some benefit, but the worst thing about Box 3 training is you will never know, because it has not been designed to be evaluated.

Validate Box 1 – Evaluate Box 2 – Ignore Box 3

Box 1 training is the most important type of training and development activity. One only has to consider again basic, airline pilot training to understand this point. So it makes sense to validate this training to ensure it is working effectively and efficiently. Testing should be carried out on a sample of Box 1 training to ensure that employees are actually learning what they are supposed to know (eg does the pilot know the checking procedure before take off?, does the waiter know all the items on the menu?). Anyone not willing to accept validation or testing of Box 1 training is not taking the training seriously. As such it has to be moved to Box 3 where it is in danger of being terminated.

Serious evaluation efforts (eg business results measurement, ROI) should generally only be attempted for Box 2 training because it is the only training for which a measurable improvement target has been set in terms of £s cost savings or revenue improvement. This should save a great deal of time (and needless guilt) in evaluation.

The 3 Box System is simple and easy for anyone to use. However, its simplicity belies its profundity and its ability to produce clarity out of confusion and complexity. In reality it has many other potential uses. On one level, you can use it tomorrow to evaluate your existing training, while on another level, it can fundamentally alter the way we look at learning and learning strategy. Try the 3 Box System for yourself. I guarantee that anyone who understands all its implications and ramifications, will never see training or education in the workplace in quite the same way again.

TOOL 5. THE BUSINESS OBJECTIVE AND TRAINING OBJECTIVE INTEGRATOR

Purpose and use – to integrate learning and business objectives so that training is linked to the business plan.

The easiest way for trainers to position themselves as business partners (see the Learning Maturity Scale in Chapter 1) is by making sure all training objectives are directly linked to business objectives. In fact, we could go much further and suggest that everyone should see the training objectives, themselves, as integral to business performance. So what does this mean in practice? Take a look at the list of objectives below which all purport to do something about improving customer satisfaction:

1　'We want to improve customer service levels.'

2　'We want to increase customer service skills.'

3　'We want to increase customer satisfaction ratings from 90 per cent to 95 per cent.'

4　'We want to increase repeat business by 20 per cent.'

Now, ask yourself, which of these are training objectives, which are business objectives and which are both? Let us look at each again in more detail.

1　Looks like it might be a business objective as long as someone is already gauging customer service levels and the business has a clear, strategic aim to improve service levels. But there is no hint of a training objective here. There could be a hundred and one ways to improve service levels, none of which might require any training.

2　Starts to look more like a training objective because it talks about 'skills'. However, there is no suggestion as to what specific skills are required and no clear indication how this would improve the organisation's bottom-line value.

3　Looks much more specific and measurable but again no indication of what training might be required.

4　Could be a great bottom-line measure and can be converted into £ signs quite easily if we already have an idea how much of the business is 'repeat' business. But yet again no sign of a training need or objective.

Maybe we can improve on all of these by being absolutely crystal clear; both about *what* we are trying to achieve and *how* we are going to achieve it. By way of illustration, look at the following statement:

> ❝ There is a specific business objective in the current business plan to increase repeat business by 20 per cent. Estimates suggest repeat business is currently worth £5 million per annum with net profit margins of 8 per cent. Therefore a 5 per cent increase would be worth £80,000 on the bottom line. We believe complaints lose us repeat business and have

already established that 50 per cent of the complaints we receive concern incorrect orders. We have tracked the cause of these errors and will be training the staff concerned to identify and resolve the root cause of these errors. This is planned to help reduce these complaints by at least 75 per cent (ie 37.5 per cent of the total) over the next three months. We estimate this could improve repeat business by up to 20 per cent in 12 months. 〝〝

If you are now thinking that it would be difficult to *prove* all of this just remember:

- Trainers who act as business partners just aim to keep training closely tied to business objectives, not to prove their case in a court of law.

- Your training solution will have as much chance of success as any other manager trying to improve repeat business and they will not be able to prove their contribution either.

- Going through this process tells line managers you are as much an integral part of the business as they are and are doing everything you can to help it improve.

Finally, remember, it is quite easy to integrate a training objective with a business objective that has already been identified and measured. Trying to do it the other way around (ie deciding on your training objectives first) is extremely difficult and breaks all the rules of evaluation.

TOOL 6. THE EMPLOYEE PERFORMANCE CURVE

Purpose and use – to produce individual, baseline performance measures to gauge the performance improvement due to training.

Probably the most powerful tool of all is the employee performance curve shown in Figure 6.2 This is based on a rating scale from one to ten with ten being the highest or best score. There is a very high probability that if you constructed this curve for almost any variable (time taken, commission earned, sales, errors made) then there would be a small group of employees whose performance was deemed unacceptable (three or less), an equally small group whose performance was superior (eight or above) but with the majority just being acceptable (four to seven).

You should be able to construct this curve from existing data quite easily. If not then you can ask employees to measure themselves (eg how many complaints have you had, what was the average time taken to complete a job, etc). Once you have some data, constructing the curve is relatively straightforward.

Figure 6.2 The employee performance curve

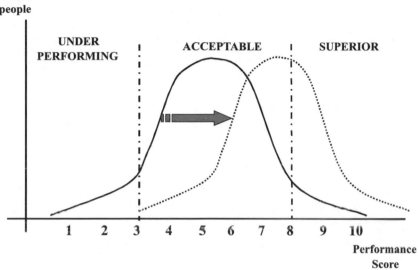

No. of
people

UNDER PERFORMING   ACCEPTABLE   SUPERIOR

1   2   3   4   5   6   7   8   9   10

Performance
Score

Let us construct a curve which measures how many calls were dealt with, satisfactorily, by operators in a call centre, in one day, using the sort of table shown in Figure 6.3.

Step 1 List all the employees in the chosen group in column A (say 100 employees).

Step 2 Put their individual score against their name in column B (90, 75, 83, 70, 92, 100 ..., etc).

Step 3 Find the highest and lowest scores (say 100 and 70 calls respectively).

Step 4 Give the highest score 10 and the lowest 1.

Step 5 Divide the difference between the highest and lowest scores (100−70 = 30) by the points on the rating scale (10) and this will give you the range for each rating (ie 3 scores will be available for each rating on the 1–10 scale). So, anyone scoring 70, 71 or 72 will get a rating of 1 on the rating scale (X axis);

Figure 6.3 Measuring productivity and quality

Column A: Employees	Column B: Calls handled and resolved satisfactorily	Column C: Rating (1 to 10)
A. Smith	100	10
B. Jones	93	8
C. Brown	70	1

73, 74 or 75 gets a rating of 2 and so on up to 97 and over getting a rating of 10. The rating for each employee goes in column C. This is their baseline score for use with the Baseline Evaluation Model.

Step 6 Add up the number of 1s, 2s, 3s, etc on in column C and plot these on the Y axis (eg 30 people achieved a rating of 5). The resulting curve should look something like that in Figure 6.2.

Step 7 Now discuss with each individual concerned whether training might help them to improve their score. The aim of the exercise is to shift the whole curve through training, as shown by the arrow in Figure 6.2.

Of course there are many organisational and cultural reasons why you might find it difficult to produce this curve. Performance measures make people more accountable for one thing. So perhaps the best way to introduce this curve is to make it entirely voluntary (but see also my book *Measuring and Managing Employee Performance* (2000) for a more detailed exposition of the issues around performance measurement and management).

However, once you have produced this curve evaluation is very straightforward. You just re-measure the variable you originally chose (in this case, calls handled) after the training. Any shift in the curve marks an improvement due to training.

Even if you do not wish to go to the trouble of collecting any data this curve can still be used to great effect in training design discussions. It is intended to move everyone away from the idea of sheep-dip training. Training the underperformers is a very different proposition to offering training to the superior performers. In reality, the most difficult group to train are the bulk of the acceptables. They can see no reason why they need training if their existing performance is deemed to be satisfactory.

Another important point worth noting here takes us back to the issue mentioned earlier that some trainers do not see the point of evaluation because they do not believe that the many variables that come into play can be isolated and measured independently. If you use the performance curve again and again, choosing different variables each time (eg next time measure the complaints from the calls or the time taken to deal with each one) then this issue is addressed very simply and very practically. However, really to make sure all variables are catered for we need one more tool.

TOOL 7. THE LOOPER

Purpose and use – to ensure learning is focused on root causes and takes into account all relevant variables.

The concept of cycles has been used extensively throughout this book. Now we are going to use the concept just once more but in a different way. Closing the loop is a key concept in evaluation but we should ensure that everything that needs to be in the loop is included.

As an example of what I mean consider this scenario, based on my own personal experience of buying a light-fitting from a large DIY chain. When I took the light-fitting out of the box at home I found that it had only one screw hole for fixing to a wall when it should have had two. So I returned it to the store and mentioned this odd defect to the customer service assistant. She was very pleasant and had no hesitation in offering me an exchange or a refund. Initially I accepted the option of a straight exchange.

Using the 'jargon' I could now refer to this interaction as a single loop, as shown in Figure 6.4 by the two boxes at the left and top of the diagram. However, it is not a closed loop, because it does not reach any real conclusions about what has gone wrong or the root cause of the problem. It is just a reaction to an immediate problem and is of little use from a learning perspective. Moreover, if the newly swapped fitting has the same defect then the customer service assistant might just suggest swapping it again.

In theory, if all the light fittings had the same defect I could have kept returning to the store and exchanging the product until there were no products left on the shelf (assuming the store assistant did not put the defective parts back on the shelf). In effect, I would be going round and round in circles. Yet any intelligent person would not take an exchanged product home without checking whether it had the same defect. We all close the loop through common sense and learning. We don't want to keep returning

Figure 6.4 Single loops do not help the organisation to learn

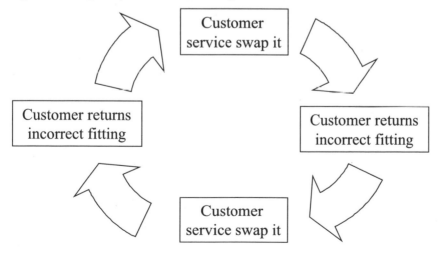

to the store. But what about the customer services assistant and the company that employed her? She had been trained to offer me an exchange or refund, but was she keen to learn?

In fact, when I picked up a replacement unit off the shelf I checked the contents only to find that it did indeed have the same defect as the first one. So I mentioned this to the assistant and this time accepted a refund and decided to buy a fitting elsewhere. However, she just put both defective parts behind the counter. So the really important question here is does the DIY company have a system for resolving this type of problem? An effective system might have ensured that all existing stock would be checked for defects. Alternatively, as soon as one defect is found, the system might dictate that all products are returned to the supplier. But even these systems do not really constitute effective learning systems. They should be based on the concept of double loops.

A double-loop system does not take a simplistic view of a problem. It does not assume there is just one variable (the particular defect on this product): it looks at all of the variables that might be involved. Consider the following:

- Maybe the DIY purchasing team had mis-specified the product.
- Why don't goods inwards check that all products are correct?
- Does the supplier actually manufacture or just distribute these products?
- If so, what might have gone wrong at the manufacturing unit?
- Who designed the product?
- Was the fault in the design or the manufacture?
- What process should a customer return go through at the DIY store?
- Does anyone note the number of defective products and, if so, is a detailed description of the defect included?

A double-loop system checks for the root cause of a problem. Only when you get to the root cause can you decide whether and what training might help to solve the problem. Certainly, training the customer service assistant might help to stop the problem happening again but if the root cause is the design of the product then the product designer must be brought into the loop.

Double-loop learning is very simple to set up but is incredibly powerful and because it is a never-ending cycle it continually leads to improvements, not just today but forever.

7 ■ PRACTICAL CONSIDERATIONS WHEN APPLYING THE BASELINE EVALUATION AND LEARNING SYSTEM TO DIFFERENT INTERVENTIONS

Although this book is split into two separate parts it is actually impossible to separate the practical aspects of evaluation from the theoretical. Understanding the theoretical building blocks of the Evaluation and Learning System (Chapter 4) will inform every learning intervention you are ever likely to produce. However, as soon as you try to apply it in practice you will find that each type of training and development activity presents a different set of issues. So this chapter deals with each of the main types of learning intervention and shows how to apply the principles of evaluation. Moreover, if you follow these principles closely you will find you do not have to evaluate very much or very often, in practice.

DO AS LITTLE EVALUATION AS IS NECESSARY

However, if you have arrived at this chapter without reading all of the earlier chapters then do not be surprised if you do not fully understand the approaches illustrated here. You might also have to revisit your expectations. If you are expecting to find lots of examples of data collection, questionnaires, surveys and feedback sheets in this section then you are going to be disappointed. There will be no recommendation here that you have to evaluate every piece of training in great detail.

Of course, in theory, we should always be aiming for perfection if we subscribe to a philosophy of continuous improvement. In practice, though, you have to be wary of losing sight of the main purpose of evaluation, which is to help the organisation to learn how to improve. If you think evaluation is an end in itself or a way of justifying the existence of the training department you will find that your evaluation efforts will soak up an inordinate amount of resources.

Anecdotal data will often provide the best insights into whether some training is working well or not (eg asking new employees whether their induction programme provided them with everything they needed and helped them to settle in). It does not always require a completely scientific approach. If one employee says the induction programme was a waste of time then you and the organisation need to start learning from this. One way to do this would be to ask two more employees from the same programme what they thought. If they were satisfied you now have to decide whether it is worth spending any more time and money just to produce a larger sample size. The chances are you have much more demanding priorities to attend to.

EVALUATION INFLUENCES DESIGN

On the other hand, if over 50 per cent of new employees thought the induction programme was a waste of time then you do have a serious problem with the design of the induction process. You need to look at it again in some detail. So evaluation is always a matter of judgment and a case of balancing priorities with resources. Listen to what the evaluation evidence is telling you and act accordingly (in accordance with the Plan Do Check Act cycle – see Chapter 2). But remember, evaluation is subject to the law of diminishing returns so always start with a very small sample size.

With these provisos in mind, this section is intended to deal with any practical questions you might have for evaluating any learning intervention. Each section deals with its particular type of training in a very straightforward manner and should be self-explanatory. They also aim to offer specific recommendations where appropriate. This is in keeping with the aim of reducing the level of ambiguity and not confusing the reader.

Before you continue though you should at least have an understanding of the 3 Box System (see Chapter 6) because this is a key element of this chapter. Some training, for example, cannot easily be ROI-d (eg induction), so being able to choose the most appropriate method of evaluation is very important. Whereas, with less tangible developmental activity (eg leadership), evaluation will significantly affect the design of any programme.

In fact, if you have read through this book in the sequence in which it is presented, you will already have learned that the answers to most evaluation problems are usually to be found in the design stage rather than during any post-event, assessment stage of any learning activity. Clarity of purpose and specific objectives are the key to effective learning and evaluation. So this chapter is really about how using the Baseline Model and the Learning System will usually result in very different design solutions for business-focused learning needs.

EVALUATING THE MAIN TYPES OF LEARNING INTERVENTION

Now, in order to make these sections as easy to follow as possible each one follows a common format and structure, namely:

- **Purpose** – what is the purpose of this particular type of intervention and what issues does this raise? Without a clear purpose evaluation is impossible.

- **Which Box?** – of the 3 Boxes, is it must have, added value or nice-to-have?

- **Measures** – how can it be measured?

- **Particular problems and difficulties** – why you might find difficulties in evaluating it and what you can do about this.

- **Evaluation report considerations** – how might you report on this type of intervention?

7.1. Induction training

Purpose

Induction and new employee programmes are almost unique in evaluation terms. Usually they are not specifically designed to achieve any business objectives but simply to introduce new employees to the organisation, its history and its purpose. They also start from the premise that the employee has zero prior knowledge of the organisation and what it does.

If that describes your own induction programme then you need to re-think its purpose. Otherwise the remit of the induction programme becomes unclear and unfocused. Here is a sample purpose for a company induction programme:

> ❝ The purpose of our induction programme is to ensure that all employees are made welcome, fully understand the company they have joined and where they fit into its organisation. It also serves the purpose of ensuring that both they and the company are not exposed to any unnecessary risks while they are finding their feet. ❞

If this is the purpose then the content of the programme could include:

- company's history
- current size and performance
- board composition

- a view on its desired culture

- basic information on its products and/or services

- any long-term plans

- the organisation structure (and where the individual fits in).

It could also cover:

- any immediate legal requirements or regulations that must be followed

- health and safety risks and precautions

- potential areas for litigation or liability.

Of course, it could also include an induction at departmental level for the individual to be fully inducted into their new role but this should be regarded as a separate part of the induction for evaluation purposes.

On some induction programmes it is tempting to include some skills development (eg basic selling skills, how to deal with difficult customers, etc) but again, this should be treated as a separate learning activity (and will be covered under one of the other sections) and regarded as requiring a different type of evaluation; even if it takes place at the same time as the induction.

Which Box?

Induction programmes, as described here, should normally be Box 1 if you are taking it seriously. This means that new employees should be fully inducted before they start working in their new job. They should not be allowed to speak to a customer, for example, until they have been approved to do so. In effect they have to 'pass' the induction programme before they are allowed to start working.

If no one wants to take induction this seriously then it will slip into Box 3 very quickly. In practice this would mean that managers put new employees to work and send them on induction at a later, more convenient date to suit their own needs. Once it is in Box 3 though the time and cost of running the programme becomes the main concern because no one is too worried about the outcomes from the programme.

Measures

As induction is about ensuring that employees' first impressions of working for the company are as positive as possible, induction is one programme where a level 1 reaction questionnaire is quite appropriate. What did they immediately think of their induction? Did it answer all of the questions they had? Would they regard their first day as a welcoming, positive experience? Was there any information that they regarded as superfluous?

Normally, induction is also, primarily, a knowledge-based programme. If you think it is important that all new employees learn something about the original founders of the company then a level 2 test question should be set to ensure they have bothered to listen to this information.

Particular problems and difficulties

The most obvious problem with evaluating induction programmes is that there is not much point trying to ascertain pre-programme knowledge. Obviously, all new employees will have gained some prior knowledge and first impressions during the recruitment process. Some of this might be inaccurate or misleading so it is normally just easier to start with a 'blank sheet'.

Hewlett Packard used to tell all new employees about the founders of the business, Bill Hewlett and Dave Packard, and how they built their first product in a garage in 1939. I could easily accept that this sends a very positive message about their values and a sense of continuity from the early days of the company but who knows how important this information really is? What difference does it make to a new employee? What effect does it have on the business? Is it still important now that HP and Compaq have merged?

Regardless of how you evaluate training it is highly unlikely that you would ever be able to demonstrate a clear connection between this sort of induction and business performance. Yet we can all understand how important an organisation's values are and how these can be imbued and reinforced through effective induction.

This is precisely why induction will only ever be taken as seriously as the importance we attach to it. If the CEO thinks this information is really important in terms of employee engagement and loyalty then it will only be seen as important if some senior managers are seen to be supporting it. Either they should be involved in the induction programme or at least be seen on the company induction video. Induction is as much about hearts and minds as it is about where to find the toilets and coffee machine.

Try not to be tempted to include too much information on the induction programme. Each element should be subjected to a rigorous TNA and enough time allowed for each element. Also, try not to have too many different objectives behind the induction. Anything that does not satisfy the original purpose should either be discarded or included in a separate event, despite the obvious pressures to reduce costs and keep employees away from their work for as short a time as possible.

First impressions can always be misleading and this is particularly true of induction programmes. New employees do not actually know which information is important and which is not. They may also suffer from being bombarded by too much information all at once; in which case the evaluation might suggest that the programme content be staggered.

As with any programme, regular evaluation should ensure that the content is constantly reviewed in terms of its relevance and topicality.

Evaluation report considerations

Attendance on a Box 1 induction programme should be mandatory for all new employees on day 1. Therefore, the only acceptable target is 100 per cent attendance. You also need to show a percentage satisfaction rating and aim for at least 90 per cent. Any testing ought also to have a minimum target of at least 75 per cent correct answers in order to be credible.

7.2. Regulatory and compliance training

Purpose

Probably the most straightforward of all training is that designed to satisfy a legal, statutory or regulatory requirement. It also usually forms a significant part of the training budget. Obvious examples would be passing an examination to sell financial services (eg the Certificate for Financial Advisers: CeFA) or obtaining a certificate to drive a forklift truck. Any stipulation that an accredited qualification is required to do a job would also put the training into this category.

No doubt some of those working in the financial services industry before qualifications were required would argue that a qualification in itself will not guarantee that holders perform their duties more effectively. This may be true, and any performance issues should be picked up through the performance management system (see Chapter 6). However, this argument is of academic interest only, because the need for the qualification is not open to debate. The requirement has already been set by a higher, external authority, and it just has to be accepted.

Which Box?

All training under this heading automatically goes into Box 1. It is probably the best definition of what Box 1 training is all about: minimum standards, a necessary qualification, risk avoidance; in short, a real 'must have' in every sense.

Measures

This is probably the simplest evaluation measure available: the achievement of the qualification will suffice. For those who pass, the training must have achieved its objectives.

Where there is to be no actual qualification, however (eg no certificate of accreditation from an examining body), you have to decide whether attendance on the programme is itself sufficient to satisfy the need (eg diversity training to satisfy current legislation or a governmental stipulation).

Particular problems and difficulties

Failure to obtain the qualification could be due to any one of a range of possible causes. Were they the right people for the job? Do they have the necessary ability and commitment? Assuming that most trainees do gain the required qualification, it would be difficult for any unsuccessful ones, or their managers, to suggest that the training itself was ineffective. The pass rate will have already clearly demonstrated that the training is doing its job properly.

The only real potential problem with any compliance/regulatory training occurs when no qualification is stipulated. For example, a government department might stipulate that all employees must attend a discrimination-awareness training programme. Physical attendance on the programme might be deemed to be enough to satisfy this declared need. However, if someone takes the department to a tribunal with a claim for discrimination, will the training be seen as effective? The organisation needs to take the training as seriously as any external body (ie a tribunal Chairman) might view it.

Evaluation report considerations

As long as the qualifications are a requirement of the job then the evaluation report should establish:

- Which jobs require which qualifications?
- How many employees are involved in these jobs?
- How many gained the qualification at their first attempt?
- The total/average costs of providing this training.
- Staff turnover in this group and the training costs associated with this.
- The extra costs incurred as a direct result of re-training those who fail.

7.3. Product and technical knowledge training

Purpose

There are potentially two main purposes of product knowledge training, although we use 'product' in the broadest sense here to include 'service' if you are a service-based organisation.

One purpose is to provide employees with just enough information to enable the organisation to operate. This might include teaching them the basic function, features, benefits and limitations of the products/services your organisation produces. So, for a mobile phone company this would include whether the phone can produce video messages, battery life and e-mail capabilities. For an ambulance service it would describe what constitutes an emergency and what call-outs would not qualify for a response.

Technical training is very similar. What technical knowledge does a photocopier maintenance and repair operative need? What does any employee need to know about the internal e-mail system?

Another purpose might be to provide employees with more and better information than that provided by your competitors. This is meant to generate a competitive advantage. So the customer services assistant in the mobile phone company is trained to understand the advantages of the tariffs, when compared to a competitor's. The ambulance service operator learns how an ambulance can deal with two calls to improve efficiency and response times.

Which Box?

For the purposes of operating effectively this training would go into Box 1 provided it is agreed that testing will take place to ensure a minimum standard of product/service knowledge.

If the training is expected to deliver measurable business benefits then it should fall into Box 2 and you should now look at 'Performance training'.

Measures

Product knowledge should be very straightforward as long as you are clear about what knowledge is required. A simple test should suffice, with a pass mark.

Particular problems and difficulties

This is likely to be probably one of the biggest categories of training in terms of time and money spent but it is easy to waste money. It is always tempting to give more knowledge to employees than they really need to do their jobs. Direct, customer-facing staff may need to be able to answer questions and complaints very quickly but other staff may just need to know where to find the information. So you should be especially careful when you are deciding what level of product/technical knowledge an employee should have.

How often, for example, do customer advisers in a motor insurance department need to know about specific exclusions on a policy? Apart from knowing that they exist, how much detailed knowledge do they need? Especially if the system holds this information and can flash it up on screen when necessary for a particular policy. If you are having to train high numbers of staff then it is well worth defining knowledge requirements in this much detail and depth.

Knowledge should be considered from the two perspectives of critical and non-critical: Box 1 training is very important, but not all of it is critical. Commencement dates and any age limits on an insurance policy are critical pieces of information because they might mean someone is driving a car without proper insurance. However, the exact model of car (eg CD or CDX), while important from a premium calculation perspective, may not be critical in terms of risk management or the customer's well-being.

Making a case for product knowledge as Box 2, added value, training can be quite difficult. In effect you would be hypothesising that a greater knowledge of insurance policies is more likely to help to sell them. If you think about this in some detail then you could equally conclude that telling a prospective customer all about the exclusion clauses on a policy might just as easily put them off. The only way to resolve this would be to try and compare sales in two teams with different knowledge levels and hope that there is a direct correlation between sales and knowledge. This could be more trouble than it is worth. It is a great deal easier just to put it in Box 1.

Evaluation report considerations

Knowledge, when measured, is easy to report on. With 100 trainees who have an average test score of 95 per cent there is a knowledge gap of 5 per cent. The test score on critical knowledge should, of course, be 100 per cent. Alongside this should be the costs of achieving the required standard. If imparting knowledge is very expensive, because the trainees are low in ability, then maybe there needs to be a change in the recruitment specification.

7.4. Competencies and NVQs

Purpose

When competence and NVQs (national vocational qualifications) were introduced into the training field over 15 years ago they were meant to be a distinct and positive move away from the old 'time served' approach to employee training and apprenticeships. They marked a significant shift in focus to the ability to do a job to the required standard. It should not matter how long someone has been working in a particular job as long as they can demonstrate they are competent. From such a worthwhile and common sense starting point it is a pity that both competence frameworks and NVQs have become an administrative burden. Nevertheless, the aim of assessing someone's competence to do a job remains perfectly valid.

Which Box?

Normally all competence and NVQ activity, by definition, would be in Box 1. There is not much point exhorting employees to gain NVQ qualifications if they do not have to have them for their work. Similarly, why put managers through competence development if they do not have to reach a minimum standard of competence?

Measures

I am reluctant to suggest any new measures in this category because I am only too aware of how much laborious effort has already gone into NVQ and competence assessment. NVQs are self-validating in the sense that once someone gains the qualification the training objective has been achieved. This is particularly true of level 2 NVQs which are the nearest approximation to a traditional apprenticeship. However, we now know that this does not satisfy level 4 evaluation and provides no indication of business benefit. Consequently, I would recommend that an attempt be made to correlate NVQs with business performance. Are fewer errors made or fewer customer complaints received from NVQ qualified staff? Are they any more efficient? If there is no apparent correlation then the whole NVQ structure should be re-considered.

Assessing management competencies is a completely different matter, however, and will never be an exact science. In fact the amount of effort needed to assess multiple competencies can often make it seem as if the cure is worse than the disease. If you look again at Chapter 6 on performance you will see that there is no reason why competencies should not be assessed against a simple 1–10 scale. As long as those assessing can articulate the difference between one score and another (eg what does the person have to do to turn a 5 into a 6) then a competence curve along the lines of the performance curve can be produced. However, it should be viewed alongside the performance curves for the same group to ascertain whether there are any connections between the two.

Particular problems and difficulties

The main problem with NVQs is that they have never achieved the credibility they aspired to as a solid and robust indicator of someone's ability to do a job. Yet they are still a fundamental building block of the government's national training policy and many public sector organisations are 'encouraged' to support them. From an organisational perspective the number of NVQs achieved will only ever be an input measure even though one would like to assume that those organisations promoting NVQs should be more effective as a direct consequence.

Level 1 and level 2 NVQs are not that problematic from an evaluation point of view because the skills and knowledge are basic and mostly observable. This is particularly true in manual trades such as the construction industry but, even in the call centre and hospitality industries, customer service skills are relatively easy to observe and assess.

As soon as you move up to level 3 (usually involving some supervisory content) and above, into the management arena, the picture is much more complex and many other factors come into the equation.

Evaluation report considerations

As with all evaluation data the key word is credibility. If senior managers see no direct connection between competence measurement and business performance then producing a report revealing that competence levels have risen will attract no great interest.

It is probably better, therefore, to regard competence as an issue of risk avoidance and consign it to Box 1. Then any reporting should be couched in terms of 'all managers have demonstrated competence in health and safety procedures' or 'litigation risk has been minimised by ensuring minimum competence standards in track maintenance'.

7.5. TQM, problem solving and other specific improvement techniques and disciplines

Purpose

This section would include Pareto analysis, cause and effect (or root cause) analysis, statistical process control (including that of the Six Sigma variety) and any other tool that is designed with a specific purpose of solving a problem or improving a variable that has already been measured (eg defect or scrap rates). All of these tools are trainable at almost every level of employee.

Which Box?

The reason I have put these tools under the general heading of 'total quality management' (TQM) is that they are best introduced as part of a systematic and continuous drive for improvement. They should follow the principles of the PDCA cycle where the starting point is to plan to improve an existing business measure. For this reason they should ideally be put into Box 2 because evaluation will be built in and there should be a chance of showing some ROI.

However, you may decide to train staff in these techniques on a totally, ad hoc basis. You could also provide training that is totally detached from the workplace or any real measures. If this is the case then you could do this training in Box 1 and make sure you test the trainees understanding of how to use these tools.

If you do not follow either of these two options the training will fall into Box 3 which would sadly be a great opportunity missed.

Measures

The measures should actually be designed into the programme. Teaching someone Pareto analysis (the 80:20 rule) can easily be designed around some existing business measures (eg how much business comes from the top 20 per cent of customers).

Particular problems and difficulties

These are all simple tools and techniques but Six Sigma is a very sophisticated version of statistical process control. There is nothing wrong with more sophisticated techniques and approaches, such as design of experiments, but the more sophisticated the technique the greater the intellectual demands on the trainee.

Also, introducing these tools without a systematic framework in place will severely limit their use and effectiveness. In general terms, the greater the maturity of the organisation the greater the probability that they will work well.

Evaluation report considerations

Steer clear of reporting on the numbers trained in any of these until such time as you can see some real results. As evaluation should be built into the design of this training there should be plenty of results to report on.

7.6. Management development

Purpose

This section is meant to include anything that comes under the broadest definition of 'management development' (eg planning, project management, supervisory modules) but specifically excludes management competence frameworks which have their own section (7.4). However, this section is also designed to make you stop and take a fresh view of something that has been taken for granted for far too long. In fact, if you look anywhere for evidence that management development, of any type, produces results you will realise just how little evidence exists. That is mainly because 'management development' rarely has a clear purpose.

Which Box?

Management development can be put into any of the three boxes but any development activity without a clear purpose always slips into Box 3. The challenge for management developers is to design their programmes to fit into Boxes 1 or 2.

Measures

If we use a module on 'planning' as our example then we could choose to put it in Box 1 by making it mandatory for all managers to have achieved a minimum standard of planning ability. We can then specify what knowledge they need (eg Gantt charts, critical path analysis) and test them on this knowledge using a questionnaire designed specifically for the purpose.

However, their skills could only be gauged by asking them to complete an exercise (eg produce a Gantt chart) and having an 'expert' decide whether it reached the required standard.

Putting the module in Box 2 requires some baseline measures. These could be agreed for each module (eg average project costs or lead times) or a set of business measures (eg costs, rework, quality) could be used for evaluating a set of modules over an agreed timeframe (three to six months)

Particular problems and difficulties

The biggest problem with management development is the very notion that it is a generic subject, that all managers need a particular set of skills or knowledge. An alternative mindset, or paradigm, suggests that all managers are unique individuals, with unique strengths and weaknesses and have to work in a variety of contexts. Being specific about the business needs, the development needs of each manager and the performance measures to be used will normally resolve any problems associated with poor definition at the LNA stage.

Evaluation report considerations

Business measures will speak for themselves but most organisations like to have a quick healthcheck on their management population at regular intervals. A credible and convincing report takes some designing. Minimum standards need to be defined for each manager, eg an ability to plan properly. If 100 managers need this ability then the healthcheck should indicate what percentage currently have it. This will, of course, change regularly due to staff movements and turnover.

7.7. Soft skills

Purpose

'Soft skills' face similar difficulties to 'management development' but even more so. The first real issue is the false dichotomy between 'hard' and 'soft'. Why, for example, do we call 'listening', 'empathising' and 'counselling' soft skills and yet refer to selling or cost control as hard? An ability to motivate, communicate and perceive reactions in others are key elements in all of these. More importantly, whether or not we continue to promote a distinction, surely the goal is the same: improved performance?

If the purpose of your soft skills programmes is the skills themselves then you will not be seeking a business improvement. Whereas if the main objective is to achieve better results then your soft skills interventions can only be gauged against that purpose or criterion.

Which Box?

The majority of soft skills training currently practised falls into Box 3. While everyone agrees it would be beneficial for managers to exhibit increased soft skills no one takes them seriously enough to put them into Box 1 because that could mean removing those managers who could not meet the standard and continued to treat their staff very insensitively. There is also a nagging doubt that the most empathetic managers may not be the most effective in terms of their team's performance.

The best box for soft skills though, rather ironically, is Box 2, where clear measures are agreed. Soft skills are actually very important because they are usually critical to encourage employees to think creatively and innovatively. However, that creativity and innovation have to be focused on value creation.

Measures

An obvious measure for soft skills in Box 2 is the number of ideas generated by a team that are implemented. Ideally these ideas will have a clear, measurable value attached. Employees generally do not come up with ideas if their boss is completely lacking in soft skills.

If you take this training seriously enough to put it in Box 1, however, then you need to assess soft skills. So do managers listen to their staff? Why not ask the staff to provide the necessary measures before and after. A 1–10 scale, as always, can be used for this purpose and is probably as accurate as any other, supposedly more sophisticated, approach. However, you must act on any unacceptable scores, otherwise the issue slips back into Box 3.

Particular problems and difficulties

The main problem with soft skills development has already been highlighted under 'Purpose'. A simple principle that 'soft is hard', ie soft skills should lead to hard results (and even a subliminal message that the soft skills are often the hardest to acquire) should send some very clear signals to anyone who asks for or attends soft skills programmes.

Evaluation report considerations

The soft skills of the management population tend to reflect and reinforce (or, conversely, undermine) the organisation's culture. Blame cultures do not encourage soft skills. Equally, though, managers who think soft skills mean 'be nice to your staff' have missed the point. At the end of the day employee feedback (perhaps through the employee attitude survey) will tell you whether managers seem to be demonstrating soft skills and hard measures will tell you whether they are working.

7.8. Coaching

Purpose

The expansion of the coaching market has been exponential in recent years and yet if you ever ask two coaches to define its purpose rarely do you get the same answer. It is not my intention here to get into a semantic debate about what is and is not coaching, or where the boundaries might lie between coaching and counselling. Moreover, I am going to make no attempt to define coaching in terms of inputs or methods (eg how to run a coaching session or what coaching models to use). Instead, as with every other type of learning intervention, we are only interested here in the potential outputs. The activity of coaching someone is only as good as the results it achieves. Even this, though, is a statement that many coaches would not accept.

Some coaches believe their purpose is individual development or life enhancement (as with life coaching). This may well be a worthwhile objective and some organisations might sponsor this sort of activity, but the sort of coaching we will concentrate on is coaching for organisational performance improvement.

Which Box?

Coaching can fall into Box 1 or Box 2 depending on the needs of the individual coachee. If the coaching is intended to bring someone up to a standard (eg coaching them on being able to run a business meeting) then it will be Box 1. If one of the objectives is improving their team management capabilities then the performance figures for the team will be suitable for Box 2.

Measures

There is no specific problem with using measures for evaluating coaching even though the coach may well focus on developmental needs (eg confidence building, assertiveness). This is another good example of where the 'soft is hard' principle should be followed. If the coach and coachee both start with a hard result in mind it will guide and inform their discussions (eg 'do you think your team are not achieving their targets partly because they are not listening to the advice you are giving them?').

Another point worth noting here is the added value question. One coach, involved in a programme that was being evaluated, suggested that the objective of the MD they were coaching in a not-for-profit organisation was to 'maintain their funding at £1 million against a threat of a 15 per cent reduction'. This might sound like an added value measure but it is not. Hanging on to funds does not, of itself, add value. Doing more with the £1 million or even doing only 10 per cent less with a 15 per cent cut in budget, however, could both be described as added value measures. Until the coach and coachee accepted this there was no basis for a coaching discussion around improvement.

Particular problems and difficulties

One problem that coaches regularly fire at me when they try to evaluate is the whole concept of pre-measurement. How can they determine what to measure, in advance, when neither they nor their coachee knows what is likely to happen as a result of the coaching? Coaches (but more often counsellors) suggest that the 'journey' should be at least as important as the destination and that having a fixed destination in mind, at the beginning, might hinder the whole learning process.

As someone who coaches on a regular basis I can sympathise with this view. I ask many questions and explore all sorts of avenues with clients in a search for solutions and results. Nevertheless, there is a very simple question that all coaches need to ask themselves right at the beginning of any coaching relationship: how was the need for coaching identified? In reality, it will often be a senior manager, who cannot fathom how to manage someone, who calls in a coach to see if they can unearth any issues that need to be resolved. The obvious question to ask such a sponsor is 'What will success look like?' or 'What indicators will move if we resolve these, as yet unspecified, issues?'

There will always be a temptation for a coach to enter into an open-ended arrangement. Good coaching is about listening much of the time so why would any coach want to pre-determine an outcome just because the evaluator says they have to? There is some validity in this view but any organisation that pays for coaching still has a right to ask what they get for their investment. More importantly, if the organisation will not accept a qualitative answer then the coach should enter into the contract with his or her eyes open and the tools required to do the job to the specification laid down by the customer.

Evaluation report considerations

In Appendix 6 is a simple form that is currently being used as part of the evaluation plan for a pilot coaching programme for small and medium-sized enterprises (SMEs). It is designed to follow the clear evaluation principle of pre-measurement. As with all good evaluations, not only does the data have to be available from the start, it needs to be in a format that can be turned into a meaningful report at a later date. More important still, it starts to inform the learning process itself. This is a form that the coach has to address at the very beginning and there is a great deal on this form for the coach to consider, not least of which is the actual performance scores to be used. With this sort of data, even on a subjective assessment, we have the basis for producing a performance curve (see Chapter 6, Tool 6) both before and after the coaching programme.

It is also worth considering exactly who is the real subject of the report.

- Coaching as a technique – does it work?

- Are the coaches, themselves, effective?

- Do the coachees perform better as a result?

These are three separate and very different questions.

The first looks just at the technique itself. This is a bit like asking how good is the surgeon's scalpel? Well, it needs to be sharp and sterile but once those simple conditions are satisfied we are less interested in the scalpel than the ability of the surgeon. Moreover, if the operation subsequently fails it is more likely to be due to the surgeon than to his or her tools.

As regards assessing the coaches themselves, there are already professional coaching bodies that are trying to establish some professional standards in the face of many independent consultants offering a coaching service. One of these coaching associations approached me to undertake an evaluation of the ROI on coaching by their members. When I informed them that ROI meant £ signs they decided not to proceed with this and instead commissioned an academic study. This may well produce a report that highlights what some of the key constituents of 'professional' coaching are believed to be but without some clear results, in much harder terms, they may well struggle to convince, whoever it is that they think needs convincing, about the benefits to be gained from coaching.

7.9. Leadership

Purpose

Leadership could be covered under management development (section 7.6) but it is a big enough subject in its own right. It is also a very popular area for training activity. Of course, on one level, the purpose of leadership development is clear: to develop better leaders. But what exactly does that mean? It is not the intention of this book to explore the wealth of literature on leadership simply because the evaluator asks one simple question. By better leadership do we mean better results? Are results the ultimate purpose and if so, how can any leadership intervention be designed around that purpose?

If results are not the purpose then what is? Transformational leadership might be required to bring about fundamental change in organisations but the ultimate aim is still to produce an organisation that delivers the best results possible.

Which Box?

Unfortunately, leadership often falls into Box 3 by default. It would be great to have better leaders but no one makes leadership ability a prerequisite for senior management posts. One only has to look at the number of senior managers who seem to possess no understanding of leadership, never mind the skills needed to be a great leader, to realise that while there is a great deal of talk about leadership development there is precious little evidence that it has made any significant difference. While it stays in Box 3 it is not worth trying to evaluate and it is unlikely to be seen by delegates as anything other than something they think makes their cv look more impressive.

Measures

There is no magic formula for measuring leadership so any intelligent attempt to assess it has an equal chance of success. Whether we like it or not senior appointments will always be filled on the basis of a judgment (or a variety of judgments from different directors) as to a candidate's apparent leadership qualities. A detailed assessment and analysis of all the various elements that we believe constitute effective leadership might provide more detailed data but will they actually produce better leaders who get better results?

Particular problems and difficulties

The main question here is the most fundamental one: can leadership be developed? There has always been a huge debate about whether leaders are born or made and an equally huge debate about the distinction between management versus leadership. I would add to this the more practical question of whether you can make a difference to anyone's leadership potential by sending them for a limited number of days on a leadership programme. If leadership development has any chance of success it has to be viewed in the long term and is more likely to result from clever succession planning and finding the right opportunities to test leadership potential than it is to do with sending managers to expensive management schools.

Evaluation report considerations

Really, the most important aspects of leadership reporting are outside the scope of this book. Talent spotting and tracking leadership potential over a significant period is probably going to be the best way of reporting. Specific leadership interventions will only be one small element of the overall picture. The board will certainly want a system in place that gives them a high level of confidence that the right quality of leaders are coming through the organisation and are being given every opportunity to develop their full potential.

Maybe leadership will always be a highly subjective area and views will always differ. Consequently, producing masses of data is unlikely to be a wise investment of time or resources. A much simpler, and probably more accurate, approach is the building up of a detailed picture of someone's track record, both in terms of performance and managerial style.

7.10. Teambuilding, outdoor development

Purpose

Having discussed the peculiarities of leadership development it is probably appropriate to make this next section focus on some of the very popular teambuilding and leadership programmes run as outdoor activities (although we will look at the more extreme types of such activities under a separate section: 7.14). With respect to organisational performance the purpose of outdoor development is often, at best, unclear and, at worst, extremely tenuous.

Some outdoor development providers would state quite categorically, with the blessing of their customers, that their programmes have nothing to do with business measures and are only focused at the individual and team level. If that is the case then evaluation is not appropriate. If you are happy with an act of faith approach to development that will be fine as long as your Chief Executive shares that act of faith and the business is doing well.

Which Box?

It is difficult to see how outdoor development can go into any box other than 3, especially if the only form of validation is likely to be the happy sheets from the delegates. Box 3 activities are often the most enjoyable from a delegate's point of view, probably because they are seen as a 'bit of fun' rather than a serious development exercise with serious consequences.

Any outdoor or team development specialists who want to put their activities in Boxes 1 or 2 can do so but the whole ethos of these activities does not really lend itself to seeking a tight focus and clear measures. That is not really what they are designed to do.

Measures

Happy sheets do not constitute a valid measure, so unless the programme is designed for Box 1 or 2 purposes it is probably advisable to just accept that it will always go into Box 3, which makes any serious attempt at measurement pointless.

Particular problems and difficulties

Of course, attempts are regularly made in outdoor development to undertake post-training assessments. Delegates are asked, some weeks or months after the event, whether they believed that the outdoor event had any effect on them and their work. Of course, the more positive respondents will say that it has and point to specific examples that they would attribute to the training. As this breaks the first rule of evaluation though (ie no pre-measurement) it is of little use. The delegates could equally have read something in a newspaper, following the event, which led them to produce a better result at work.

Outdoor development, by its very nature, is highly experiential. It takes place away from the workplace, in unusual surroundings, offering activities that may have no direct relevance to someone's day job. In addition, many providers ask delegates to attempt some quite risky, physical challenges. The excitement of abseiling or crossing a river on a makeshift raft is likely to stay in the memory much longer than a regular management meeting in a stuffy office. As a result, strong emotions and reactions can be aroused. Delegates can declare that they have undergone some fundamental change in outlook or behaviour.

There are several basic problems with outdoor development, however. If it is detached from real, workplace situations then it is impossible to evaluate it until delegates are back at work. Also, the team on the programme may well not be working together afterwards, so any improvement in team spirit or team cohesion is subject to the normal vagaries of team dynamics. The other main problem is it that outdoor development, arguably more so than most other training programmes, tends to involve intensely personal experiences (either positively or negatively). This could be of some benefit but evaluation is not about personal effectiveness, per se, it is about the impact that person has on the organisation in which they work.

Evaluation report considerations

The only issue worth ascertaining here is whether outdoor development represents a better return on investment than other methods? However popular it might be, and even if you think it gets results, someone might ask whether the money could be better spent elsewhere. Any training and development that leans more towards the 'act of faith' school of management is always more susceptible to any changes in beliefs from new CEOs and finance directors.

7.11. E-learning

Purpose

It is probably fair to say that the fevered interest in e-learning over the last few years has already passed its peak. So we can now afford to take a rather sober look at what the real purpose behind e-learning was. Before we do though we need to define what we mean by e-learning.

E-learning is really a misnomer; if anything it should be called e-training. We don't call reading a book 'print learning', or watching a training video 'tape-learning'. The 'e' is really just the method of delivery and provides no greater guarantee that learning will occur than any other medium, including 'classroom learning'. The possible purposes for any training and development are the same as those we established in Chapter 3, regardless of how it is delivered. E-training might be a more efficient delivery method (although this is by no means assured) but this is a peripheral issue concerned with cost savings and has nothing to do with the essential purpose of the training. So we should not be blinded by the glare given off by the white heat of the latest technology.

Which Box?

You cannot put the whole content available on any organisation's e-training system into one box. You have to look at each individual piece of e-training available on the system and then make a decision as to which box is most appropriate. This throws up an interesting perspective: that of the individual trainee. There may be a training module on how to produce a profit and loss account, for example. For a trainee accountant this would fall into Box 1 whereas for a line manager it would be Box 3. E-training has to follow all the principles and rules that we have set out throughout this book.

Measures

The measures will be dictated by the choice of box and individual circumstances just as with any other piece of training that we have explored and discussed.

Particular problems and difficulties

The main selling points held out by e-training providers were that it was a more efficient (eg no need to pay travel expenses and hotel costs for trainees) and more flexible (ie the participant could learn at their own pace at a time that suited them) delivery system. It was as though the technology itself offered such great advantages that the 'e' became the most important, even the sole, selling point.

Of course, however successful it might have been, e-training could never really, fully deliver on its promise. It could not possibly meet the level of expectations that were created by the hype surrounding the launch of the first e-training systems. There are several good reasons why. First, the apparent savings were often swallowed up in setup, infrastructure and development costs (see Appendix 3 for some real examples) and second, the only way to gauge its effectiveness was to measure how much people had learned.

Another serious issue is the maturity of the organisation, which we covered in Chapter 1. There are some very immature organisations, in learning terms, who have very deep pockets (some parts of the financial services sector fit this description very well). So they buy in what they believe is the state of the art in e-training systems but make no other organisational adjustments to encourage people to make the best use of it. No one owns staff development and no one evaluates the results. The best examples of e-learning will actually come from organisations who see it as part of a wider knowledge management strategy and only organisations approaching Stage 6 on the Learning Maturity Scale will be in a position to do that, both culturally as well as organisationally.

What has happened in the meantime is that many experienced trainers, who realise that each of us has our own learning styles and preferences, have been vindicated in their reluctance to jump on the e-learning bandwagon. Some people prefer a book and others like the support and reassuring tones that only a tutor can provide. So now we have seen a move back to a more blended approach to training, where the benefits of different methods and styles can be used to best effect.

Perhaps the most serious problem of all with e-training though is that the content is pre-designed, in advance. This means that it cannot be based on an individual LNA. This tends to make the content very generic. It also means that the content is designed with no pre-measurement in place.

We have all learned that technology has its place in the training and development armoury but it is certainly no universal panacea.

Evaluation report considerations

One subject that needs a mention here is the advent of learning management systems (LMS) that have become part and parcel of e-training projects. Again, they tend to be more like training management systems, with an emphasis on measuring the participant's usage of various modules, how many times they hit a site and how long they spend on it. None of this measures learning. Only those LMSs with validation tests built in are able to do this.

7.12. Evaluating education (qualification based programmes)

Purpose

It might seem a rather ridiculous question to ask but have you ever stopped to think what the purpose of education is? In general terms no one would be against the idea of education and the present UK government have a rallying cry of 'education, education, education'. It might help to have some definition of what we mean though, so please visit Appendix 5.

Of course, there could be much debate on these definitions but this is not at issue here. The issue is what can and cannot be evaluated in education. As always, this brings us back to the original purpose. So what, for example, might be the purpose behind supporting employees to pursue MBA qualifications or even a professional qualification such as an accounting or purchasing diploma?

The number of managers with MBAs has grown exponentially over the last 20 years or so but what impact has this had on the organisations that employ them? Alternatively, does an accountant really need a diploma to do their job properly? Or is the purpose of this diploma just a professional 'meal ticket'? Many people work in the HR and training fields with no diplomas or specialist qualifications at all. Would there be any purpose in trying to ensure all training managers had a particular qualification?

Which Box?

By now you should have realised just how important the 3 Box System is in evaluation. An MBA can go into any of the boxes. To go into Box 1 the MBA has to be seen as a minimum standard for a particular job. This could be a complete act of faith that MBAs are worth having but once it is in Box 1 everyone knows that they must get the qualification if they want to move up through the management career route. This is not the same, of course, as saying that managers need the knowledge and skills that are supposed to result from an MBA. The piece of paper becomes the only requirement.

Box 2 MBAs should be designed around work-based projects and some measures have to be set up as a baseline. By doing this you will notice that the MBA now moves from being a pure qualification to something that is specifically designed to add value. Of course, there would still be a great deal of education and teaching of the theories of management but the criteria for success would be value-based.

In practice most MBA programmes would just sit in Box 3. No one's job is dependent on having the MBA and no one makes any attempt to link the degree to a specific set of business objectives. However, in such circumstances it would be illogical to expect the company to support employees pursuing MBA programmes.

Measures

If you were trying to measure the benefits of all the money you spend on education the very least you should measure is the success rate. That is, if you spend £1 million for trainee accountants to pass their exams what is the pass rate (without resits)? This is only an input measure but you would still do well to manage this figure as much as you can.

For Box 1 education programmes (think of a financial services compliance regulation) the only acceptable score, of course is 100 per cent. Anything less indicates a very serious risk factor (ie legal liability and the chance of being fined or sued).

Particular problems and difficulties

If you do not bother to make a distinction between what constitutes education and training then it is very difficult to have a clear policy. What do you do when an employee tells you their plans to study for an MBA and then enquires about funding? Of course, you can just have a policy that is a blank refusal but what signal would that send? Equally, agreeing to some qualifications and not others sounds inconsistent, even discriminatory.

The more you think about this the more it makes sense to have a clear and coherent policy statement. For what it is worth I subscribe to the view that any organisationally sponsored training, development or education should have a clearly demonstrable business benefit in mind. I would not sanction personal development activity where there was no obvious business connection.

There is nothing to stop your organisation sponsoring education programmes as an act of faith but such schemes have a habit of being challenged when times are hard. I was asked some years ago by IBM to help produce some figures to justify $50 million worth of MBA programmes. I told them that unless the programmes had been designed with ROI in mind they were never going to find the figures to post-justify this expenditure. They should either continue 'speculating' in such programmes in the hope that they make a difference or change their policy completely. At the time they were caught between two schools of thought that were irreconcilable and they had not managed to forge a coherent policy from this standpoint.

Henry Mintzberg, a very famous and well-respected professor at McGill University in Quebec has criticised MBAs, arguing that management should be taught only to people who already have management experience. After examining the careers of 19 Harvard

MBAs who had made it to the top (40 of America's 100 largest companies were run by MBAs at the time) he found that 10 subsequently ran into big difficulties: generally, their company went bust or they lost their job. (See also Mintzberg (2003).)

Evaluation report considerations

As we move into an era of human capital management (see (2004) *Human Capital Management – One Stop Guide*) simple reports on the number of staff with qualifications might be required as a legal reporting requirement. However, any attempt to correlate company performance with educational attainment levels would obviously be welcome.

7.13. Corporate universities

Purpose

Corporate universities, as a major development in the training field, have many similarities to the advent of e-learning. They became a 'flavour of the month' when many corporations decided that their old, centralised training centres were looking tired and needed revitalising. The main purpose, if there was one, behind the notion of a corporate university was that it should foster closer links between research institutions and companies needing to innovate. They were also seen as a way of tying up with an academic institution that could offer external accreditation for many management training programmes being run in-house. Inevitably, as with many fashionable developments, some organisations followed the trend without being too clear about what they expected in return.

One very large UK retailer set up its own 'university', albeit really just as an umbrella organisation for its existing training efforts. There was no attempt to signal a fundamental shift in thinking or emphasis. Another client of mine visited the annual corporate university conference and exhibition in America and reported that not one of the case studies on the conference programme made any attempt to show how the corporate university was contributing to business results.

Which Box?

As with e-learning it is impractical to try and lump the whole edifice into one particular box. Each separate item of training undertaken under the guise of a corporate university can be put through the added value scanner individually (see Tool 3). However, at a policy level, the fundamental question has to be asked: is the university intended to add real, measurable value or not? The concept of corporate universities, just as e-learning, has already passed its peak and this must be due, to some degree, to the fact that the institutions are being treated as Box 3 enterprises. Look at this quote from Jack Phillips, the leading US commentator on evaluation, in the *Chief Learning Officer Magazine*, February 2004

> **❝** While executives pursue corporate universities for different reasons, their long-term viability has recently come into question. Many corporate universities have suffered severe budget cuts. Some have been disbanded. Still others have been outsourced. **❞**

Measures

Again, as with e-learning, usage tends to be measured but this is of little use to an evaluator. There is nothing unique about corporate universities to make their measurement any more of an evaluation challenge than any other type of training activity.

Particular problems and difficulties

When advising on the setting up of a corporate university in Europe in the late 1990s the main problem for me as the evaluator was asking what particular benefit the university idea, itself, brought. The training programmes planned were no different to those that would have been run by a typical training department. Yet the infrastructure, communication, branding and PR that often goes with a corporate university all cost significant amounts of money. So what do the glossy presentation aspects contribute? Does it matter whether a university accredits management programmes?

We may yet see the concept of corporate universities revisited in future years but next time around the formula may be very different and is more likely to be founded on a clear business case through the use of evaluation and ROI techniques.

Evaluation report considerations

Any corporate university is going to be a significant investment. While there is board support for the idea there will not be too much pressure to justify every bit of expenditure and usage rates may suffice. However, it is advisable to have some harder data available should the need ever arise. In the retail example quoted above the whole university was literally just about to be launched, with some fanfare, when the finance director at the latest board meeting enquired whether anyone working on the university project had produced any hard figures to justify the investment. All of a sudden the name of the game had changed and the university planning team had some very serious thinking to do.

7.14. Public and not-for-profit sectors (including government and civil service departments, local government, NHS, education, police, charities)

Purpose

It might seem out of place, in a chapter divided into *types* of training, to suddenly come across a section on a whole (and some would say very disparate) *sector*. The reason for this is that defining 'value' in the non-commercial world presents its own practical problems. In any commercial organisation value is relatively easy to define (although it is not as straightforward as some public sector trainers seem to assume).

Value is defined, in the round, by all of the stakeholders. Commercial organisations have many stakeholders to satisfy, including the Chairman, the CEO, the board, line managers, employees, shareholders, city and financial analysts, investment fund managers, customers, the environmental lobby and society generally. In practice though, as long as they produce an acceptable profit and stay within the law their stakeholders will be satisfied. The public sector probably has as many stakeholders but they also have to consider the views of taxpayers, council members, voters, regulatory bodies, government ministers and civil servants.

In short, all organisations have a multitude of stakeholders all with their own perspectives and opinions as to what constitutes value. Therefore, trainers need to establish what the consensus is on value before they can design any training. The purpose and value of the training should be synonymous. Moreover, the training can only be evaluated against a clear definition of value. If a council 'values' saving money by cutting library budgets the trainer can only produce training that helps to achieve this end, even though they may do their best to ensure the service from the library remains the same.

Which Box?

Once the purpose or value is established then training in the public sector can use the 3 Box System in the same way as any commercial organisation.

Measures

Public sector organisations do not necessarily have any different measures to any other organisation. However, many of them are service-based and we can measure service in a variety of ways. If a council empties your refuse bins we could measure their efficiency (eg bins emptied per £1,000 spent on refuse collection), their service level (eg how often do the bins get emptied) or by the quality of the service (eg how often is your bin missed or how much mess is left on the road?).

Particular problems and difficulties

The public sector presents one particular problem associated with the use of ROI calculations. That is, the 'gross benefit' figure tends to have to be related to cost savings. As public sector organisations rarely have a price mechanism or a profit motive they generally cannot put a sales or revenue increase into the gross benefit part of the equation.

However, there is one way to resolve this particular issue. Hospitals in the NHS may not make a profit out of patients using their beds, but there are clear costs associated with every patient occupying a bed and receiving treatment. If, for example, the average total cost of caring for a patient from admission to discharge is £5,000 then every extra patient treated within the existing budget is worth £5,000 worth of value. This will not show up as extra revenue but the trainer can use this figure to produce an ROI calculation to demonstrate the benefits of their training to improve the effectiveness of patient care.

Of course the other main issue with service delivery organisations is that the quality of the service is often a very subjective matter. How well do social services 'clients' feel they have been treated? What do school pupils think of their educational standards? Do a GP's patients feel that he/she is sympathetic to their ailment? The evaluator should not be afraid of such subjective measures, indeed they should be happy to embrace them, but they have to put clear measures in place and agree with their boss and other stakeholders what success looks like. Do GPs, for example, have to be concerned about showing sympathy to their patients or is their job simply to make them well?

Evaluation report considerations

The main considerations on reporting tend to be due to the 'political' complexity of such organisations. Local authority elected members, boards of trustees, community leaders and the like may have very different agendas. So, for example, diversity may be more of an issue for a local councillor representing a ward with significant ethnic diversity but of little interest to a line manager who just wants to get their job done. Whether this really presents any unique or more difficult issues than reporting in commercial organisations is debatable. If council members are interested in knowing how many days training were completed last year that is no different to an executive director asking the same question. The main principle to follow, in any organisation, is to educate your audience as much as possible as to what constitutes a meaningful and reliable evaluation report.

7.15. Unorthodox events

Purpose

It might seem contentious to have a catchall section that groups together many other methods of intervention. It might even be provocative to suggest that, somehow, these are the unorthodox approaches. Who am I to act as the arbiter of orthodoxy, and what do I mean by 'unorthodox events' anyway? Well, anything that does not follow the orthodoxy of analysing business needs and then individual learning needs. In effect, the 'method' used, itself, becomes the most important aspect of the exercise, rather than any effective learning that might result. A good, recent example would be the 'Fish' approach (see Lundin et al (2000)).

Unorthodox approaches often result in the syndrome of a pre-prepared solution looking for a problem. The most popular methods that tend to come under this umbrella include things like Neuro Linguistic Programming (NLP) and 360° feedback. Here, the techniques used are assumed to have some beneficial effect on the trainee but often there is no attempt made to establish any business measures in advance. At the most extreme end of the unorthodox events scale come horse-whispering (promoted at one time by Manchester Business School) firewalking and other attempts to bring about a fundamental shift in someone's thinking, behaviour or attitudes through an intervention or significant event.

We could debate whether there is any merit in any of these methods but all the evaluator wants to know is where the evidence is that they produce any value. We often hear anecdotal 'evidence', from both the purveyors of such practices and some of their customers, of remarkable experiences and even stories of how transformations took place, back at work. However, if there is no clear purpose at the beginning of the exercise (eg what do we expect you to learn from firewalking and what will you do differently as a result?) then the first rule of evaluation has already been broken.

Furthermore, this is the only category in this chapter where often the whole point of the exercise is not to have any pre-determined, clear purpose in mind at the start. These methods are designed to unearth or unleash latent talents and capabilities or produce a whole that is greater than the sum of the parts, one of the aims of the Gestalt therapy that underpins some of these methods.

Maybe, if no pre-determined purpose is the aim, it is unwise to try and cater for these practices in a book that sets out to establish the orthodoxy of evaluation and learning. However, as we shall see under 'problems and difficulties' below, there are many other strong arguments against using any method that does not have a clear purpose. Moreover, there is no reason why NLP should not be used to help someone achieve a pre-determined objective. Once that objective is established and measured, then the 'technique' can be evaluated in exactly the same way as any other section in this chapter.

Which Box?

Without any clear purpose any intervention must go into Box 3. It is worth reminding ourselves though that being consigned to Box 3 does not guarantee that the intervention will add no value. The firewalking may or may not 'work'. No one can say though whether Box 3 activities are working or not because they were never designed to be measured. However, what we can say about Box 3 is that there is a lower probability of this intervention being effective or adding value than if it had been designed for Box 1 or Box 2 purposes.

Measures

Of course, there is always the possibility that some measures will be attached to some of these interventions. Probably the most obvious example is 360° feedback instruments, which produce a great deal of data and graphical charts if produced on a piece of proprietary software. Seeing a shift in a 360° chart might suggest that the members of a team now view their team leader as someone they prefer to work for. This might be encouraging but it might equally suggest they are loosening their grip or going 'soft'. Regardless of what conclusions you might come to, the chart will not tell you whether value was added.

Some 360° instruments do not even work on the basis that they can produce a comparable before and after picture. If the instrument is ipsative (totally subjective with no fixed frame of reference) rather than normative (comparable with others in a given population) then there is no way of saying that the post-training individual is, in any way, better than they were before the training took place.

Particular problems and difficulties

It is probably apparent that I am not an advocate of the sort of 'unorthodox' methods mentioned here. That is probably as much to do with personal preferences as it is with a clear-headed, systematic approach to learning. I have a sneaking suspicion that unorthodox methods do not, by and large, offer a viable alternative to systematic improvement. If they did, then this book would not have been written. In 25 years of working in the training and development field I have found that a systematic approach, clearly linked to business needs, offers the best chance of achieving significant value.

There are also several other serious considerations, however, for those who advocate unorthodox methods:

- Any method offered to an organisation is competing with a range of other options. Getting anecdotal evidence from a small percentage of those subjected to such methods cannot hope to compete with a method that aims to improve every trainee (and what about those trainees who, literally, burnt their feet?).

- As evaluation has, heretofore, been absent in the vast majority of organisations it was often a lottery when decisions were made about competing methodologies (eg should we endorse NLP or not?). As evaluation starts really to take hold, lotteries in training will become a thing of the past. Evaluation and ROI will produce most of the winning tickets.

- The concept of no pre-determined objectives as a basis for a learning intervention is questionable, but there is a fallacious assumption by some providers that this is the source of great creativity and innovation. They argue that trainees can give free rein to their full creative potential when they are not hide-bound by narrow business objectives. If that is true then how is it that the car maker with the highest market value in the world, Toyota, has a very systematic and business-based approach to learning? It doesn't seem to have stifled *their* creativity.

Evaluation report considerations

We can all try different methods and some of them may be regarded as unorthodox or even wild, wacky or experimental. Every organisation can choose to use whatever methods they deem fit for the purpose. However, if that is the prevailing attitude in your training team or organisation as a whole there is a very high probability that no one will be asking for evaluation reports.

SO IS THIS THE LAST WORD?

If you have read this book completely from the beginning to the end you will now have a full grasp of the theory and practice of evaluation and ROI. The intention was to remove the confusion and misunderstandings that have dogged the subject for so many years. So has it worked for you and delivered? As always this is the evaluator's ultimate question? Is it really the last word on the subject?

I doubt it. I am sure there will be many more articles, books and debates on the subject for many years to come. Some will have a vested interest in making the subject more complicated than it needs to be. But will they bring anything new to the topic? Yes, there will be refinements, special cases, exceptions and even some fresh insights but will the fundamentals change, either now or in the distant future? As we enter the era of Human Capital Management, when everyone has complete access to enormous databases of knowledge through their mobile phone or PDA, will it guarantee that they are more effective employees? I guess not, if they choose to be seduced by the technology in the absence of a solid learning and evaluation system.

All I can do now is make sure my own last words in this book will leave the focus in future not on evaluation, per se, but where it should always have been: individual and organisational learning.

APPENDIX 1: THE TOP 20 MOST COMMON QUESTIONS ABOUT EVALUATION AND ROI AND SOME MODEL ANSWERS

I have probably been asked thousands of questions about evaluation and ROI since I started specialising in the subject. These have come from all quarters of the globe; some from academics but most from practitioners, and I have always done my best to provide a full answer. Often the questions themselves reveal that the questioner does not really understand the subject of evaluation (eg 'Which questionnaire would you recommend for …?') or they have some fixed, preconceived ideas or misconceptions in their mind (eg 'How can we do level 4 on Kirkpatrick?'). On other occasions the question is just a clear sign that the person concerned is against the whole concept of evaluation and this is just their way of voicing their objection (eg 'Of course, you can't always measure the things that really matter'). In effect, it is just a thinly veiled attempt to undermine the subject by trying to pick holes in it.

As someone who has literally spent years developing and refining his own critical questioning technique, I readily accept that asking searching questions is a very important skill. It is also a great way to learn, and many of these questions have shaped my own thinking on the subject. They have also served the very important purpose of checking the rigour of my own methodology. In fact, I would only dare to write a book that purports to be the 'the last word' on the subject of evaluation if I believed I had managed to provide a simple, practical answer to all the questions ever thrown at me.

I firmly believe there must be an answer to every question, even if we have not actually found them all yet. But there certainly is an answer to anything you may ever wish to ask on the subject of evaluation and ROI. It might not be the answer you were hoping for, or expected, or even wanted, but that does not mean the answer must be wrong. So here are the top 20 questions, the most common ones that come up again and again. Of course, the full answers to these can be found sprinkled throughout the body of this book, so here are just the summarised versions. If you cannot find your own questions in here please feel free to contact me direct, as I am always eager to learn.

Q.1. How will I ever know that it is the training that is making the difference?

A. You won't, usually. The implicit assumption here is that the purpose of evaluation is to prove that it is training that is making the difference. Evaluation does not try to *prove* anything. It simply increases the probability that training will be effective. Don't make too many demands of evaluation and never set a standard that no one else in the organisation is prepared to meet. Proving anything in business it is very difficult. It would be problematic for any single function in a business to prove that it, alone, is getting results. Just because sales look good does not mean that all the credit should go to the sales team. A large market share is not just down to the marketing team. It is just as likely that everyone in the organisation had a part to play. Moreover, if everyone in the organisation were to keep asking this question about their own efforts the organisation would sound very divisive. If you still think that evaluation should prove that it is training that is making the difference then perhaps you should read parts of the book again.

Once you start building evaluation into the design of your training you will not ask this question in future. The contribution of training designed around evaluation will be self-evident.

Q.2. How do you separate out all of the variables that might be having an influence on performance?

A. You don't. Well, at least not until you are already very good at evaluation. Statisticians do have techniques for trying to isolate variables. For example, in a production process they might want to identify whether the product is defective because of the raw materials, the speed of the machine, the way it is set up or how well it is maintained. To do this there is a whole branch of statistics called 'design of experiments' and organisations using statistical process control or Six Sigma will be conversant with it. One day you might like to look into this subject but only when you require that level of sophistication.

This question is also very similar to Q.1. Maybe you are setting too high a standard for evaluation? If you want to separate out all the variables influencing someone's performance you could be making your own life very difficult. Consider the variables that influence a sales person's performance: product quality, after sales service, the price of the product, other competitors' products, advertising, marketing, product design. The list is almost endless and somewhere in amongst it is a bit of training and development.

The more specific you are about the business need and then the individual's learning need the less you should worry about separating out variables. If you identify one performance factor as being 'lack of product knowledge' then design some specific learning effort to resolve this particular issue, but at least consider other variables that might positively or negatively impact on this at the same time.

Q.3. Should I design a control group experiment?

A. A control group in training is a group of employees who do not receive the training that everyone else receives. The basic idea is to be able to compare the results both with and without the influence of training. If you have read the answers to Q.1 and Q.2 above you can probably guess that I do not normally recommend the use of control group experiments. One reason is because you cannot normally keep an organisation still while you try to observe the change in one variable. Organisational life does not work like that: we do not have the time and we have to cope with a highly dynamic situation. Variables do not change individually, they are all constantly changing simultaneously.

The second reason is more practical. While you are running a control group that group is not performing as well as it could with the training. You might be proving a point but don't expect the CEO to pat you on the back for missing a business improvement opportunity.

The third reason though comes back to designing in evaluation. If you do this you do not need a control group.

Q.4. Training usually produces incidental benefits – how can you evaluate these?

A. External training providers who run programmes with no specific outcomes in mind usually throw this question at me. These could be NLP, creativity, team building or something similar. The whole point of this type of 'development' activity is not to have specific business targets in mind. Yet the proponents of it are quick to remark that they have seen some wonderful results from their training.

This is probably true. There will always be some incidental results from any training activity that was not planned. Even I am constantly surprised how many people I have trained over the years that come up with ideas and actions that were never envisaged as part of the original programme. So how do we capture all of these 'extra' benefits in evaluation? The simple answer is we don't.

The whole point of pre-training evaluation questions is to establish the need for the training in the first place. If these needs are specified and the training is designed to achieve the objectives set then the training is justified. Any extra benefits that accrue can then rightly be regarded as 'the icing on the cake'. However, what is the point in trying to measure the icing when the cake itself was a wise investment? This would be a waste of resources that serves no purpose.

The shorter answer is you can never post-justify a training programme. If it was not justified in the first place it should never have happened. Moreover, 'incidental results' cannot be used to justify future programmes because there is no guarantee that the same 'incidental' benefits will occur.

Q.5. How do you evaluate soft skills programmes?

A. The same way you evaluate any programme. This question is actually predicated on a false dichotomy. There is no distinction to be made between soft skills and hard skills. They should both produce a better performance and organisational improvement. Selling produces hard results but many of the skills required could be described as soft. Counselling sounds like a soft skill but it is only worth doing if the employee performs better as a result, or has less time off or stays with the organisation longer.

At the design stage of any explicit soft skills development the evaluation question is the same as with any other training activity: what is the business need and how will this training add value?

You can try to validate soft skills if you want to but you will find this is more difficult than evaluation. Testing for soft skills requires level 3 observation (eg is the manager being more empathetic with their staff after the training?), which is very time consuming and labour intensive. It also requires someone with a particular capability for analysing soft skills.

Q.6. Evaluation measures the benefit to the organisation but what about the benefit to the individual?

A. This could also be described as a false dichotomy: an anticipation of a conflict between the needs of the individual and the needs of the organisation. In practice, this is usually more an apparent problem than a real one.

Take an individual who works in IT and wants to develop their programming skills in a language the organisation does not use. Obviously they would only want to do this out of pure interest or, more likely, with one eye on their future job prospects in the market. So, first of all, why should the organisation support such training? What's in it for them?

Well, one possibility is they may have future plans to use this particular programming language; supporting this training could indeed be a recognised business need. Or, they might take the view that keeping this employee happy will mean they can retain him/her for longer. In other words, you should always check whether there is a business need. If there is then this question no longer applies, does it?

However, if there really is no apparent business need we are back to the original question of why should the business support it? One answer is simply that it should not, but there is probably a better answer.

The best answer lies in checking the perceptions of the individual concerned about the value of the training they have decided they want. Is it really of any value to them? If it is purely driven by personal interest then they should be asked to come up with the reasons why the business should pay for it. If they think it is going to help their job prospects then it is a bit like asking the business to help them to decide to leave, which most organisations would be reluctant to do.

Maybe the individual has actually misread the market though? Have they considered this? Is the job market looking for programmers in this language and how much are they paying? Would a training programme be sufficient to get them another job or do they need three years' practical experience? If that is so then they will have to leave the business to obtain this.

The same line of questioning can be applied to any type of personal training or development. Take management skills. Will a three-day course on project management provide the experience required or do people really need to get at least one successful project under their belt?

The short answer is to make sure the individual is going to receive the benefits they expect. But even then, measuring individual benefits, on their own, is of no interest to the evaluator.

Q.7. Evaluation can take a lot of time – how will I know whether it will be worth it?

A. If you mean collecting and analysing happy sheets, collating test results and running three- or six-monthly follow up surveys then this will take up an inordinate amount of time. Unfortunately, none of this constitutes evaluation, so it might not be worthwhile. This is *validation* activity (focusing only on training objectives) and is only normally recommended for Box 1 training (see Chapter 6). Even then, you should start with as small a sample as you can reasonably expect to get away with. The rule of thumb is that it has to provide you with a sufficiently high level of confidence that the training is actually achieving what it was designed to achieve (eg high levels of product knowledge).

Real evaluation should be the least resource intensive part of the whole process because this should be designed at the beginning. Moreover, it is the individual trainees themselves, and their managers, who should be performing the evaluation: this should be part of their training contract.

Finally, on the subject of whether this is all worth it, evaluation, itself, should add value. It is not an ivory tower, academic, exercise. It is also not meant to be an end in itself. It is there to improve the effectiveness of the learning process. As long as you do as little as you have to do it will be worth every penny and every minute.

Q.8. How do I cope with all the paperwork?

A. If you are producing lots of paperwork you have missed the point of evaluation. You need to re-think why you are producing so much paperwork.

Q.9. How do I cope with all the figures and statistics?

A. The only figures and statistics you need for evaluation are business figures that already exist. If your training is focused on improving the existing revenue, cost or quality measures that line managers are already monitoring then they are the people who will tell you whether the training is working or not. If you are creating new figures or setting up new data collection systems there is a distinct possibility that you have gone off track somewhere along the way. Not only does this mean you are now having to manage more data but, even more serious, no one else in the organisation owns the data you are producing. The link between training and the business has broken down somewhere.

Q.10. Who should do the evaluation and do we need a specialist evaluation team?

A. One simple answer to the first part is 'whoever the person was who said the training was needed in the first place'. That is most likely to be a line manager but if an individual analysed their own needs then they should also accept responsibility for demonstrating that the training was worth it. If either of these do not accept the responsibility they are already sending a clear signal that they have little commitment to the learning opportunity.

In spite of this, and the answer to Q.9, you might still believe that evaluation is such a new, highly specialised and important subject that it warrants the establishment of a dedicated team. This would be a bad move because it sends all the wrong signals to your organisation. First, it implies that evaluation is something that happens as a separate, detached, exercise to the day-to-day running of the operation, which is incorrect. It also takes the responsibility for evaluation (and therefore accountability for training and development) away from where it should be, which is with line managers.

The training team should only be doing evaluation as a last resort if no one else will pick up the baton. Certainly, whoever gains the expertise in evaluation should be willing to share it with line managers so they can eventually take full ownership.

Q.11. I get lots of good feedback from previous delegates and trainees so why should I evaluate?

A. It is obviously very pleasing and rewarding to hear delegates say the training was great. Sometimes you even hear stories months after the event about what they gained from it. Anyone who works in development will know this happens. In fact, the lessons imparted during the training frequently do not hit home until much later, when the trainee is faced with a particular situation where they have to employ the lessons they have learned. None of this, though, could be used as an argument to demonstrate that the training was worth doing. Every day we all learn things from newspapers, journals, TV and even conversations with colleagues and friends that may be of some use in our jobs. What would be the point in trying to evaluate all of these?

Every time you decide to do some training there should be some clear business and learning objectives at the outset. It is only these objectives that can be used for evaluation. Moreover, what about all the trainees who did not provide any feedback. How good was it for them?

Q.12. Why can't I just look at what happens after the training? Why do I need to concentrate on the baseline?

A. If you run a management programme on 'how to plan', but with no baseline measures in place, there is always a chance that some of the delegates will apply what they have learned. You could then ask how many of them had planned their work better. You could even ask them if that helped them to save money and you might get some positive answers. However, this is called 'reverse engineering': trying to make the facts suit your case.

No one is going to stop you adopting this approach but you could be made to look very silly, very easily. For example, why were these particular managers on the planning programme in the first place? Who told you they needed training in this area? Was it because they were identified as deficient in planning skills? You can only answer this if you had some measures of their performance beforehand.

Q.13. I am a training provider and my training provides all sorts of benefits including morale boosts, greater levels of motivation, team spirit, etc. How can evaluation capture all of this?

A. Firewalking, raft-building, spending nights out under canvas, etc are often organised by the training department. Whether these exercises can be termed 'training and development' is another matter. What really matters though, are the results you expect to achieve. Unfortunately, increases in 'team spirit' or 'morale' cannot be used as evaluation measures simply because they do not measure value. If the team now works more effectively as a result of the programme then this might be a measure of training benefits, but then the effectiveness of the team would have to have been measured before building the raft.

Q.14. How can I prove, beyond any reasonable doubt, that my training is working?

A. This is a book for training practitioners, not barristers. Very little, in management terms, can be proven. We are not concerned with proof but probability. If we assume (rather generously) that any training starts with a 50:50 chance of success then the question for the evaluator is how to improve this level of probability. We want it to be as near to 1 (certainty) as possible. Everything in this book has that aim in mind. It does not set out to prove anything because, from a practical, organisational viewpoint, that is an unattainable and unnecessary goal.

Q.15. If evaluation shows that my training hasn't worked it isn't necessarily my fault so why should I take the blame?

A. If this is the way you approach learning – 'Who will we blame if it goes wrong?' – then you are either in the wrong job or the wrong organisation. It is just as important for evaluation to show when training isn't working as it is to highlight success. The whole point of negative feedback is to learn from it, not to blame someone else.

Q.16. You can't put a £ sign on everything in training, can you?

A. Actually, that is both factually and conceptually untrue. First, all training has a cost (in £s) and it is only worth something if it generates some benefits (again, in £s). Admittedly, calculating the benefit in £s can be problematic (see Box 1 in the 3 Box System) but then we can look at what risk the training reduces or what minimum standards it sets per £ spent. So yes, you can put a £ sign on all types of training and the reason this is a useful discipline is that interventions that do not have £ signs attached are rarely taken that seriously.

Q.17. If my company is happy enough without evaluation why should I bother?

A. If they are happy and you are happy with this state of affairs then feel free to carry on as you are. The problem will arise when you get a new boss or new CEO who starts asking more difficult questions. What do you do then?

One of my clients, the head of learning in a large bank, was asked by their chairman 'What do we get for all this money we spend on training every year?' Once that question was asked the head of learning suddenly had a lot of work to do. In fact, it had fundamentally changed their entire job. Another training manager, who had won several awards (see Q.19), was made redundant, along with his whole department, when a new CEO took over.

It is wise to be prepared for any eventuality and the questions being asked by CEOs are getting tougher all the time.

Q. 18. We have a National Training Award/IiP accreditation/industry award – so why should I evaluate?

A. As someone who has judged national training competitions it is easy to see that once an award is offered it has to be given to someone. The organisation that wins is usually the 'best of the bunch' rather than the 'best' in any absolute sense. Moreover, hardly any judges will know anything about real evaluation so they are likely to be more easily impressed.

I have never yet met an organisation that fully satisfies the tough evaluation criteria of the Investor in People standard in over 12 years' involvement with the scheme. This has not stopped thousands of organisations being accredited under the scheme though.

It is probably about time that any training accolades and awards were given to those who provide the best evaluation evidence.

Q.19. Development doesn't happen straight away, it takes time, so how can we evaluate that?

A. Probably the best question here because it shows an understanding of some of the deeper issues surrounding evaluation. Development does present some difficulties in evaluation but they are not insurmountable. The secret is to approach development from a different angle. I could train someone to use cause and effect analysis in about half an hour. I could then establish whether they are using it immediately at work. But this picture would not tell me how well developed they had become in its use. At some point I would want to see them explaining it to their team and perhaps even other colleagues. I would also want to see them using it in more complex settings and adapting it to slightly different purposes. Ideally they should even have to develop facilitation skills to help other teams use it effectively. All this behaviour is observable and assessable so this would give me a level of confidence that the right development is taking place.

However, if we start with a series of baseline performance measures on errors, reject rates, scrap rates, complaints, rework and return after sales visits then this becomes the foundation for my training on cause and effect analysis. This is action centred learning and development. I would also want to be around to coach him/her when they stumbled, refresh some of the learning points and pick up on any areas of misunderstanding. I would only have total confidence in their development, however, if the baseline measures continued to improve and, at some stage, the person being developed suggested new baseline measures.

Q.20. Leadership is too complex a subject to be evaluated isn't it?

A. It all depends on what you mean by leadership and how you intend to develop it. If you define leadership as a set of innate personality traits and values backed up with competence then training and development only has a chance of impacting on their competence. Personality traits are in-built and values are not easily influenced. Yet measuring and assessing competence is only one small part of the overall 'leadership formula'.

'Leadership' is not a business need, per se, and never will be. This does not mean the desire for better leadership is not a valid one. Organisations that say they need leadership are really just saying 'We are not performing as well as we could if we had better leaders.' The learning cycle, therefore, tries to clarify the real business need, the under-performance question, before it tries to resolve it through leadership development.

So why not define leaders as 'those that manage to get the best results out of the organisation as a whole', regardless of their individual traits and competence, then you have the basis for evaluating leadership development.

If you consider premiership football managers as leaders it is difficult to talk about their leadership qualities without looking at their performance over several years in terms of how many trophies they manage to win. Running any organisation is a very unforgiving task for those who do not get results. Immature organisations run generic leadership training programmes in the hope that they will have some impact. Mature organisations, using the learning cycle, link developmental programmes to measured business objectives.

APPENDIX 2: A SHORT CRITIQUE OF OTHER EVALUATION MODELS

If I'm asking you to change your whole approach to evaluation then it's only fair that I should explain why I think why the myriad of evaluation models already on offer do not provide a complete solution to the evaluation problem. You don't need to read this if you just want to know what I think you should do. If, however, you want to know why I have such unshakeable confidence that this is the right way to approach evaluation and that some other approaches have just got it plain wrong then read on.

Before we look at each model in turn though here are the main distinguishing features of the Baseline Model. It:

- emphasises the principle of pre-measurement
- looks at all training from a performance measurement perspective
- pre-determines expected added value and ROI expectations, where appropriate (Box 2)
- can only work within a learning system (using the learning cycle)
- defines level 4 clearly and specifically as added value, with £ signs
- only refers to level 4 as true evaluation
- regards levels 1, 2 and 3 as mere validation
- makes a critical distinction between basic and added value
- includes ROI at level 4
- reduces the emphasis on post-training evaluation.

In general terms, as a practitioner, it would be fair to comment that none of the models produced by academics are of much use in a real-life work setting. Consequently, none of the obviously 'academic' models are included here. So how do some of the other models, at least those that make some effort to be usable by training practitioners, stack up against the Baseline Model?

KIRKPATRICK'S FOUR-LEVEL MODEL

The main body of this book already shows where Kirkpatrick's model did not go far enough in theoretical as well as practical terms. One of the main limitations is its lack of definition about what value really means. Interestingly, he has tried to address this relatively recently (Kirkpatrick (1998)) by stating:

> **❝** Results can be defined as the final results that occurred because the participants attended the program. The final results can include increased production, improved quality, decreased costs, ... It is important to recognise that results like these are the reason for having some training programs. Therefore, the final objectives of the training program need to be stated in these terms. **❞**

Despite this apparent conversion to the cause of value, I don't think Kirkpatrick believes that trying to state 'the final objectives of the training program ... in these terms' is, in itself, probably the most important step in the whole learning process. There is no clear statement here that value is the whole raison d'être for all training and development. No critical distinction is made between 'basic' and 'added' value.

Kirkpatrick's original intention was to try and demonstrate that training worked but the evaluation process itself serves a much greater purpose than this. I believe that it is the *act* of trying to put a real value on training, in advance, that enlivens the whole learning process and brings into the loop everyone involved in the subsequent value chain (senior managers, line managers, supervisors and individual employees – regardless of any departmental or functional boundaries).

If anything, rightly or wrongly, Kirkpatrick's model was usually seen as emphasising *post*-training evaluation or measurement simply because the four-levels model refers to what happens *after* the training takes place. This turns a potentially very lively learning process into a very bureaucratic and tiresome paper-based exercise. Yet trying to measure the effect of training only after the event is a theoretical and practical impossibility. Paradoxically, if you are only planning to carry out measurement once it is the pre-measurement that should take precedence.

Now we will look very briefly at the other contenders, in order of their estimated popularity, and suggest why they do not provide anything like the total solution offered by the combination of the Learning Cycle with the Baseline Model.

◼ JACK PHILLIPS' ROI MODEL

Probably the biggest contender after Kirkpatrick would be Jack Phillips (Phillips (1991)) and his five-level ROI model. This is really just an amended version of Kirkpatrick's four-level model. Phillips' main contribution to the debate was that Kirkpatrick just stopped short of the ultimate level, the actual ROI calculation itself. He therefore produced his own 'extra' level, level 5, just to complete this sum. Here is his justification for this approach:

> **❝** The four level framework developed by Donald Kirkpatrick ... does not focus directly on the ROI issue. ... Kirkpatrick defines Level 4 evaluation as the results linked to training. These results could take the form of reduced absenteeism and turnover, quality improvement, productivity, or even cost reduction. But this level of evaluation does not require a specific monetary value (cost savings) to be determined. To obtain a true evaluation the monetary benefits of the programme should be compared to the cost of implementation in order to value the investment. In effect, this process moves evaluation to the next level – Level 5 in our revised Kirkpatrick model. Thus, the fifth level of evaluation is developed by collecting Level 4 data, converting the data to monetary values, and comparing them to the cost of the programme to represent the return on training investment. **❞**

(Phillips (1996))

It is questionable, however, whether Phillips' level 5 is necessary if real, £s value has already been ascertained at level 4. If profit has increased by £1m as a result of sales training and the cost was £100K then the ROI is just a simple calculation resulting in a net 900 per cent ROI. The calculation itself does not add anything to the evaluation process. It does give you a great number to take to your boss, but I don't think it does anything to help you improve the value that your training will deliver.

Where Phillips diverges from Kirkpatrick is that his version of the model is predicated not on pre-measurement but the notion of converting training benefits to a monetary value. This might sound like the Baseline value question but it is an entirely different approach. No conversion should be required if the training is designed at the outset to impact on real value (eg meals sold in the restaurant or average spend per meal), the £ sign is attached and potential ROI calculated straight away.

The Baseline value question does not pretend what the value of the training might be; this is not meant to be a hypothetical question. Even if the results of the training are never going to be measured it is still meant to be a serious question. If we send 1,000 employees on a customer service course how much more profit will we make through improved customer service? More importantly, it demands to know who has to get involved in the learning process to actually make this happen. Phillips does not apply this rigorous test. In fact, he made the same omission as Kirkpatrick by failing to define added value precisely in terms of output, cost or revenue. Here is an example:

> **❝** Better service – Another potential benefit of time savings is better service .... As a result, there is better customer satisfaction, the value of which is difficult to quantify. **❞**

(Phillips (1983))

I would argue that that customer satisfaction is meaningless if not translated into higher sales and, as a result, it is very easy to quantify the value of an improvement in customer satisfaction. Provided, of course, that at the outset you had a clear idea of the value you are trying to add through your training, in this case increasing sales by improving customer satisfaction.

As a consequence of having the emphasis in the wrong place (at the end), both Kirkpatrick and Phillips seem to view evaluation and ROI as nothing more than a mechanistic process and that is their biggest failing in the author's opinion. In terms of popularity, Kirkpatrick and Phillips are still the most oft-quoted evaluation and ROI models. However, they do not make the connection between learning cycles, PDCA and evaluation. Neither do they ever seem to mention the concept of the learning organisation in the same context as evaluation.

HAMBLIN'S FIVE-LEVEL MODEL

Hamblin is probably the next main contender after Kirkpatrick. His model looks very similar but it also has five levels:

- reaction
- learning
- job behaviour
- organisational effects
- ultimate value.

(See Hamblin (1974)).

Immediately, though, we can see that Hamblin's first level is already post-training. There is no pre-training measurement principle enshrined here. Consequently, this model cannot be used in practice to demonstrate results and there is no sense that it is part of a learning cycle.

What is even more interesting though is the distinction made by Hamblin between 'organisational effects' and 'ultimate value'. He suggests that evaluation can take place at two, different, organisational levels: at the team (or departmental) level and then the final 'value' level. In practice this can actually happen quite often. A sales team could be trained to sell more products but this might not feed through to extra value if the price has been heavily discounted. So at Hamblin's fourth level the 'evaluation' shows good results but at the 'ultimate' level there is no greater profit.

In my experience, training departments that use Hamblin tend only ever to report on results at departmental level (even though the lack of pre-measurement makes this meaningless) and never consider the ultimate value.

INDUSTRIAL SOCIETY'S (NOW THE WORK FOUNDATION) 'CAROUSEL' OR ENDLESS BELT OF DEVELOPMENT MODEL

The UK-based Industrial Society produced its own evaluation model for those who attended its training programmes. This model comprised six stages:

Stage 1   Recognise a business need

Stage 2   Define development objectives

Stage 3   Design learning process

Stage 4   Experience the learning process

Stage 5   Use and reinforce learning

Stage 6   Judge the benefit to the organisation.

This looks more like a real challenger to the Baseline Model, despite the fact that it is not in general use. It starts with 'business needs' and is described as a never-ending cycle, which both fit perfectly with the learning cycle concept. On the basis of these two elements it is already ahead of the other models mentioned above.

However, its main weakness is its lack of definition about what constitutes a business need. It does not specify that this need must be one that will generate value, either basic or added. Moreover, its use of the word 'judge' at Stage 6 is a clear indication that the business need was not measured before the training took place. If it was pre-measured there would be no need for judgment, the evidence would be plain.

THE CIRO MODEL

The CIRO model takes its name from the initial letters of the following:

    Context evaluation

    Input evaluation

    Reaction evaluation

    Outcome evaluation.

(For details of the CIRO model see Warr et al (1978).)

It is probably on the borderline between being of academic and practical use. Some training teams profess to use it but they seem to regard it as a conceptual framework rather than a workable set of guidelines, rules or steps to follow.

It is probably one of the more sophisticated approaches to evaluation and deserves some greater attention, however, not only because it is a very comprehensive view of where training analysis should begin, but also because it covers a much broader perspective than the simple Kirkpatrick Model. Its main contribution is its focus on the context in which training and development is to take place. This is crucial in effective learning and many training teams would learn something just from considering this first step. It also highlights a key distinction between 'inputs' and 'outcomes'. For these reasons alone it should help move many trainers away from their broad brush and generic attitude to training using 'sheep-dip' or 'scattergun' methods.

As with all of the other models, however, its main deficiency is in its failure to define value, and hence evaluation, in clear and precise terms with £ signs attached. There is no distinction between basic and added value training and no sense that it should be part of a complete learning cycle.

APPRECIATIVE ENQUIRY

The final 'model' to warrant inclusion is not actually an evaluation model at all. It merits a brief mention here, however, for three reasons:

- It was used by one of my potential clients some years ago in preference to the Baseline Model.

- It has achieved some popularity amongst some OD specialists as a means for focusing on the positive aspects of change.

■   It tries, in its own way, to create value.

As an evaluation tool it has very limited potential application but as a means for unearthing opportunities in organisations it has something to offer and should be welcomed by anyone wanting to create organisational value. It concentrates on the positives and what succeeds and does not focus just on 'problems' and what went wrong. So maybe its real relevance in terms of this book is that it offers some alternative techniques to use at the value analysis stage of the learning cycle.

It is worth looking into by anyone wanting to see evaluation in its broadest and positive context and there is a wealth of information on the subject on the internet.

■ APPENDIX 3: REPORTING AND PRESENTING EVALUATION DATA AND INFORMATION

The reason that evaluation reporting is included as an appendix rather than being in the main body of the book is to emphasise to the notion that evaluation reporting is only a small part of the complete evaluation and learning picture. Evaluation is meant to be, first and foremost, a live, dynamic process. It should be totally integrated with operational management and should not be viewed as a bolt-on or a post-training report that follows on long after the learning has taken place.

Nevertheless, reporting has its place. Evaluation will mean, on occasions, the completion of forms and paperwork. When used effectively these can be very powerful but they should only be part of a total approach to evaluation and should never be seen as an end in themselves.

So, with these provisos in mind, what might an annual evaluation report look like? We can only answer that by first asking who the report is for.

▌ DESIGNING REPORTS WITH THE 'CUSTOMER' IN MIND

Why report?

There are many reasons for wanting to report on the results or benefits of training. It can tell everyone that the money is being well spent. It can justify the existence of the training team. It can even suggest that this is such a wise investment that it is worth allocating more resources to it. You will notice that all of these tend to take a very positive view of what the report might reveal.

But reports should also paint a true picture and be prepared to feedback negative results as well as positive. Maybe levels of commitment by senior managers are not as they should be? Perhaps some employees do not take training and development seriously.

A report should not be viewed as an end in itself. We produce management reports to provide management information. Management information is that which enables managers to make informed decisions. A report should not be the same as reading a glossy Sunday magazine, superficially interesting but of little substance or practical import.

To whom do we report?

We could decide to report to all or any of our stakeholders. These will include the board, managers, the training team and other employees. But what about shareholders and customers? Do shareholders want to know that they have invested in a company that invests wisely and tries to get the most value out of the potential of its people? Would customers be interested to know that train drivers have passed rigorous tests and high standards of training before being allowed to drive?

Each of the stakeholders may well have their own agendas and vested interests. Maybe we would do well to report to all of them in slightly different ways.

Of course, reporting has some serious, political implications. Who wants to report bad news or evidence of ineffectiveness? Two of my regular pieces of advice to training departments embarking on serious evaluation for the first time are:

- Manage expectations as well as you can. Do not offer to provide an evaluation report unless and until you are confident that you have the systems in place to produce some good results.

- Don't shoot yourself in the foot by proving that your training is not working. Only report on the best results at first.

In simpler terms, if you know exactly what you want your report to achieve you cannot go too far wrong.

What do we want 'customers' to do with our report?

My own main reasons for producing an evaluation report include:

- demonstrating the effectiveness and added value of learning in order to attract more resources

- integrating learning and business operations

- establishing learning as a key source of business, competitive advantage

- reinforcing a continuous improvement philosophy by showing improvements in learning and performance year on year

- articulating a vision of what a learning organisation is and what it can achieve

- addressing any weaknesses in the way the organisation is performing through learning.

Once the purpose of the report is clearly understood you can then start to produce the report itself.

ANNUAL EVALUATION REPORT

The basic structure of the report can be based on both a historical and a forward-looking view, ie training and development that has already happened and any plans for the following year. There will be some factual data, diagrams and tables but there should also be a narrative that discerns changing trends in learning and how these are being addressed by the organisation.

Your first report should include some preamble to explain the overall framework and approach used. This could say:

PREAMBLE

We have installed a combined learning and evaluation system since January 2005 and now all training and development needs are subjected to a rigorous process based on some simple principles and a series of challenging questions before any resources are allocated.

It is our intention to make the learning and evaluation systems integral to business operations over the next two to three years once the effectiveness of the whole system is proven.

Progress has to be monitored and some indicators given that the systems are being used properly and are becoming embedded. These could include those listed in the box at the top of page 143.

Of course the next main component will be how much was actually spent. This is most easily and most effectively represented by the 3 Box System. The titles of the boxes can be changed to suit the terminology or language used by your organisation. For example, Box 1 might become the 'foundation' or 'core' box. In a bank, Box 2 could be referred to

LEARNING AND EVALUATION SYSTEM INDICATORS

- All internal customers have been trained in the learning system and evaluation models.

- All appraisal/personal development planning/performance review forms have been modified to include the 3 Box System (see below) and pre-measurement objectives.

- 90 per cent of all training spend is now subjected to the system before approval.

as the 'cash generation' box. You should seize any opportunity you have to raise the acceptability and credibility of the system. Graphics always help with impact of course (see as an example, Figure App 3.1).

The 3 Box split of the budget also shows a target for spending. Realistically, there will always be a demand for some 'act of faith' events that will end up in Box 3 but this should always be minimised. The detailed information for producing this sort of chart will come from categorising all training activity during the TNA or appraisal process. However, there is little point presenting detailed information to the board. All they need to know is:

- Is the organisation at risk because of insufficient training?

- Is training spend being used wisely?

- Is a systematic approach being used?

Figure App 3.1 Example of 3 box system: total training spend

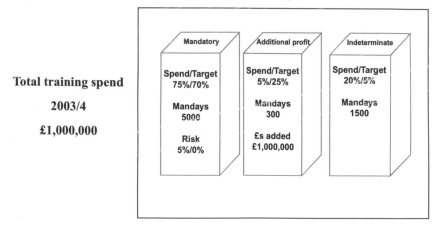

Total training spend

2003/4

£1,000,000

Mandatory	Additional profit	Indeterminate
Spend/Target 75%/70%	Spend/Target 5%/25%	Spend/Target 20%/5%
Mandays 5000	Mandays 300	Mandays 1500
Risk 5%/0%	£s added £1,000,000	

E-LEARNING PROJECTS

Many trainers will have had some involvement over the last five years or so in e-learning projects. These are usually relatively large financial investments and, as such, require reporting. The first e-learning report should establish a clear purpose: is e-learning meant to provide training more efficiently, thereby enhancing everyone's learning opportunities, or is it something to do with knowledge management? Figure App 3.2 is designed to establish some of the implicit assumptions and misconceptions about what e-learning can achieve. These graphs pose the questions:

- Will e-learning speed up the learning process (broken line) when compared to traditional training (continuous line)?

- Will e-learning reduce training costs (line of xxxs) compared to costs of traditional training (dotted line)?

Figure App 3.2   What is e-learning meant to achieve?

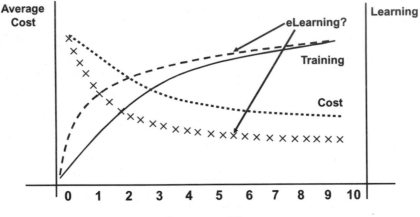

Output over Time

If these are the objectives then real data should be collected to produce real graphs. This requires testing of trainees (level 2) using both traditional and e-learning methods of delivery. Assuming e-learning does achieve quicker knowledge acquisition then the cost curve should also show savings. Unfortunately, e-learning can have significant start up costs as we can see in Figure App 3.3.

These are real figures taken from a client some years ago in the very early days of large e-learning projects. The only figures that really matter here are highlighted showing cumulative costs and benefits. The benefits were supposed to be cost savings on venue costs and other expenses and it was anticipated that these would cover the costs of the e-learning set up after three years. However, using the ROI formula, the actual payback

Figure App 3.3 E-learning start-up costs can be significant

		Scale 1	Scale 2	Scale 3					
		Oct–98	Apr–99	Oct–99	Apr–00	Oct–00	Apr–01	Oct–01	TOTALS
	PCs (per site, Sc1=40, S2=20, S3=2)	160	220	114	0	0	0	0	494
	Servers	6	11	57	0	0	0	0	74
	Sites	4	11	57	0	0	0	0	72
	Coverage @50staff/1PC	8000	11000	5700	0	0	0	0	24700
	Costs								
	Servers	180000	330000	855000					1365000
	PCs	320000	440000	228000					988000
	Master class suite	500000							500000
	Commissioning/marketing	140000							140000
	Development	496000	900000						1396000
	Staff and other costs	235000		235000		235000		235000	940000
	Hub	130000							130000
	Network maintenance	100000		100000					200000
	TOTAL COSTS	2101000	1670000	1418000	0	235000	0	235000	5659000
	CUMULATIVE	2101000	3771000	5189000	5189000	5424000	5424000	5659000	
	Benefits								
	Training days available p/6mths on LN		0	19200	45600	59280	59280	59280	59280	301920
4	Useage as 20% of existing total training		0	6600	6600	6600	6600	6600	6600	39600
	Savings @ £100 per day	100	0	660000	660000	660000	660000	660000	660000	3960000
	CUMULATIVE SAVINGS		0	660000	1320000	1980000	2640000	330000	3960000	
5	Plus added value @ 1% of Drama costs pa				1670000	0	1670000	0	1670000	5010000
	TOTAL SAVINGS+AV		0	660000	2990000	3650000	5980000	6640000	8970000	
	ASSUMPTIONS								

1	P&BT current revenue is £4M – 20% conversion to LN is £0.8M plus 20% of remaining £16M at BBC is £3.2M – total £4M
2	£4m equates to a maximum of 20000 training days pa @ £200 per day transferred to LN
3	Conversion of extra £3.2M of training to the LN costs £0.9M
4	Max training days possible 6600/£4m = 33000 for £20M so useage max 6600
5	Drama costs £167M pa

Figure App 3.4 E-learning payback took five years, not three

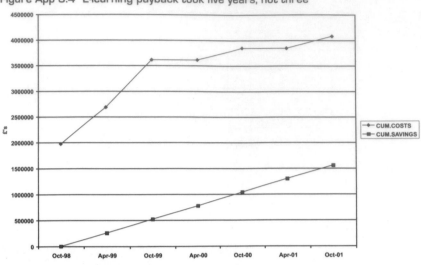

period was calculated and is shown in Figure App 3.4. This shows that the two curves, cumulative costs and savings, did not intersect (ie there was no break-even) within three years. It would take another two years of savings to achieve any payback at all. This was eventually the basis on which the e-learning project was given the final go-ahead.

APPENDIX 4: AN EVALUATION ALGORITHM – FOLLOW THE SIMPLE STEPS

Figure App 4.1 An evaluation algorithm

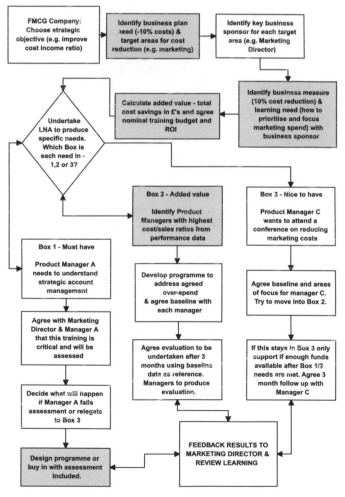

■ APPENDIX 5: KEY TERMS IN EVALUATION AND LEARNING SYSTEMS THINKING

Here are some working definitions, from an organisational management perspective, of the terms used in this book. There is meant to be a clear and practical distinction between each. There is no attempt here to replace the *Oxford English Dictionary*. You may disagree with the definitions offered but the intention is to try and ensure that, at least while they are used in the book, there is no unnecessary misunderstanding or confusion.

Added value

Value can only be said to be 'added' when costs fall, revenue rises and quality improves or at least remains constant. A simple but very powerful concept and one that will appeal to any Chief Executive or Finance Director, once they fully understand it (see also 'cost effective' below).

Balanced business scorecard

The concept of a set of balanced measures, rather than just financial data. Popularised, some would say over-promoted, by Kaplan and Norton (1996) but the concept was around for a long time before the proprietary product.

Book value

A company's book value is total assets minus intangible assets and liabilities such as debt. A company's book value might be more or less than the market value of the company. It can also be the net amount shown in the accounts for an asset, liability, or owners' equity item.

Bottom line

The ultimate arbiter of value: did the company make profit that can be banked? What is left when all revenue and costs have been taken into account.

Commitment

How long is a piece of string? Without real commitment to learning you will struggle with evaluation. So how do you gauge real commitment? Articulate value. Make managers accountable for learning reinforcement. If they pass these tests you have commitment.

Continuous learning

Something we do anyway, every day, eg by reading a newspaper or watching TV, but in an organisational context this should be 'continuously learning how to improve the performance of the organisation'.

Continuous improvement (sometimes referred to as 'never ending improvement')

Both a philosophy and a way of life involving a set of models and tools. It means never accepting the status quo and always believing that things can get better. Encapsulated in the simplest but most powerful tool of all, the PDCA cycle.

Control group

An attempt to isolate a variable (eg training) to establish its effect. In training terms it means training one group of employees (eg sales skills for salespeople) whilst observing another 'identical' group who do not receive the training (ie the control group). The aim is to show that the group, which is trained, does better than the control group.

Cost effective

There is no such thing as cheap or expensive training when one considers cost effectiveness. Low-cost training that is ineffective is a waste of money. Effective training that could be achieved with lower costs is also wasting money. Only the right combination of both can be called cost effective. A better concept though is added value.

Development

A longer-term view of training which builds personal capabilities as a result of iterative, experiential learning. Development time cannot be short-circuited and has to be spent in the workplace. According to this definition most 'development' programmes would only qualify as training programmes.

Education

Knowledge acquisition and assimilation as evidenced by the achievement of a qualification.

EFQM

The European Foundation for Quality Management, which purports to be a model for organisational excellence. An EU-sponsored organisation that also runs the European Quality award. A very sophisticated model that spells out everything that is implicit in the PDCA cycle and more. Predicated on a social democratic view of the world which includes an organisation's responsibility to society, not just its customers and shareholders

Evaluation

The concept and/or process of trying to put a value (£s) on (training and development) activity. Not to be confused with validation.

FTSE 100/250

The Financial Times shares indices for the top 100/250 quoted companies in terms of market capitalisation.

Inputs/outputs

Inputs are time, cost and effort expended. Outputs are the results the organisation requires (cost reductions, more products delivered, more revenue, better quality service).

IPR (intellectual property rights)

IPR is a generic phrase encompassing intangible property rights, including, among others, patents, trade and service marks, copyrights, industrial designs, rights in semiconductor chip layout designs, and rights in trade secrets.

Learning

The application of skills, knowledge and experience in the workplace.

LNA (Learning needs analysis)

A broader view of the traditional training needs analysis (TNA). TNA tends to look at individual needs while LNA looks at organisational needs.

Line of sight

Imagine a telescopic sight on a rifle: can you see the target in the distance or are there many obstacles in the way. If we improve employee satisfaction today can we see a distant improvement in sales as a result?

Loops

Closed/single/double. A closed loop system is one where there is feedback (eg did that new marketing campaign work?) so that we can learn. A single loop system looks at one specific variable (eg was the advertising copy any good?). A double loop system looks at all of the possible variables (ie competing products, current market conditions, price, advertising copy and quality of advertising, etc).

Market capitalisation

The product of a company's share price multiplied by the total number of shares issued by that company. The simplest measure of the value of a company at any point in time.

Measures

Measurement in management will never be an exact science but a distinction can be made between activity measures (those that only measure activity without any output, eg sales visits per day), performance measures (number of sales per visit) and added value measures (profit on those sales).

PDCA

Plan, Do, Check, Act: a simple but powerful continuous improvement cycle based on a plan to improve something already measured. Goes back as far as the 1920s (Walter Shewart) but made popular by the quality guru Deming. Requires a context with an open, no-blame culture in order to work successfully.

P&L

Profit and loss account, the basic building block of accounting systems and usually reported on monthly and annually. A fundamental management tool used every day. Never tells the complete story about how the business is doing but will always concentrate the minds of operational managers. Hence a very powerful focus for training and development discussions.

Plc

A publicly limited company whose shares are traded on the stock market.

ROI (return on investment)

A simple financial formula for calculating the net, percentage return on an original investment – in this case a training investment:

$$ROI = \frac{Gross\ benefits - Costs}{Costs} \times 100\ per\ cent$$

This formula demands a £ sign on both variables. The costs are relatively easy to define and measure but putting a £ sign on the benefits presents some practical difficulties. Nevertheless it can always be done, even if there have to be some assumptions clarified at the outset.

Organisation development (OD)

The conscious act of installing an organisation-wide learning system to improve and create organisational value.

TNA (training needs analysis)

An attempt to discern the training an individual needs to perform their job to the required standard. A TNA has to be linked to a business needs analysis. (See also LNA.)

Training

Delivering the skills and knowledge required for an employee to perform their role as cost effectively as possible.

Validation and validity

An assessment of whether training objectives were achieved (eg can you now use a spreadsheet?) as opposed to evaluation, which asks whether a business objective was achieved (eg do we produce the accounts more efficiently now?). Validity asks whether the training is relevant to the needs of the organisation but does not put a value on it.

Zero defects

A term closely allied to 'continuous improvement', which describes a philosophy of searching for perfection. No error or defect is acceptable. Perfection is never reached but the pursuit continues nonetheless as a means of continuous improvement. Intended to stamp out complacency but at the same time to act as a motivator.

APPENDIX 6: COACHING AGREEMENT

The form in Figure App 6.1 is already in use on a coaching project and the design was based on all of the principles espoused in this book. It is worth noting that the Box 1 section refers to 'critical' objectives and Box 3 allows for other, non-measurable, objectives which will not actually be included in the evaluation. This is how minor modifications can be made to ensure the tools are adapted to the particular purpose and context.

When this form was first used some of the coaches who signed up to the scheme found it very difficult to complete some of the key areas of the shaded section of the form. This, in itself, was quite illuminating. Were they finding it difficult because the measures are difficult or because they have never before tried to tie their coaching skills to specific objectives?

One coach remarked that he was having great difficulty with two particular managers who would not agree to any clear objectives for the coaching sessions. He was doing his utmost to help them but I advised him that this form was as much a measure and test of the coachee's commitment as it was a means to undertake an evaluation. If they did not buy-in to the objectives then they had not bought in to the whole coaching process. He was therefore asked to raise this matter with his MD. This is exactly how this form, and evaluation, is meant to be used in practice.

As with any evaluation form though, it should aid and guide the process and not create unnecessary barriers. So perhaps a piece of sound advice is always to work through the completion of any forms with those who have to use them. We should not assume that they are as easy to use as we would like to think.

Figure App 6.1 Coaching agreement

Company name		
Coach name		
Sponsor	Usually the line manager responsible for the coachee	
Client name	Coachee's name	
Objectives		
Box 1 – Critical		
Box 2 – Added value		
Box 3 – Non-evaluated		
Trigger dates	3 and 12 month dates for evaluation	
Added value:	Variable measure	Performance score
Output/productivity	Insert actual baseline measure	6
Cost	Insert actual baseline measure	5
Revenue/price	Insert actual baseline measure	6
Quality/customer service	Insert actual baseline measure	7
Skills gap	Specify	4
Knowledge gap	Specify	5
Number of sessions		
Regularity of sessions	State frequency of sessions (eg fortnightly)	
Schedule of sessions	Dates and times sessions agreed	
Procedure	The client and coach will meet at [a pre-arranged time and location]. Please indicate any arrangements that may be necessary for telephone coaching if applicable	
Changes	Re-scheduling or cancellations of appointments should be done at least XX hours before the planned date otherwise full payment is due	
Additional support	Please state any additional support you intend to provide such as interim telephone sessions, write up of sessions, etc	
Extra time	You may e-mail or call me between scheduled sessions if you need urgent advice, have a problem or want to share a success with your coach	
Problems	If you have any concern with the way the coaching is working, please let your coach know as soon as possible. For our work together to be effective, you must alert your coach to any problems	
Formal review	State when formal review will take place (this should be at least every six sessions)	
Termination	State arrangements for termination and any fees due on early termination	
Confidentiality	The coach recognises that anything the client shares with them is regarded as confidential, whether it is business or personal information. The coach undertakes not to, at any time, either directly or indirectly, use or disclose any information that the client shares with them during their sessions	
Coach's objectives	To act as a detached, independent thinker enabling the client to address their objectives by helping the client to work out for themselves how to achieve them and the actions they will take.	
Nature of Coaching	The client is aware that the coaching is in no way to be construed as psychological counselling or any type of therapy. Coaching results are not guaranteed. The client enters into the coaching with the full understanding that they are responsible for creating their own results. The client must be committed to achieving their goals and active in working towards them between sessions.	

Client has read and agreed the above

Client signature _____ Date _____
Coach signature _____ Date _____
Sponsor signature _____ Date _____

■ REFERENCES

Accounting for People Report. October 2003 (see www.accountingforpeople.gov.uk).

ARGYRIS, C. (1999) *On organisational learning*. Oxford: Blackwell.

EDVINSSON, L. and MALONE, M. (1997) *Intellectual capital*. New York: Harper Business.

HAMBLIN, A. C. (1974) *Evaluation and control of training*. Maidenhead: McGraw-Hill.

HOPE, J., FRASER, R and HORNGREN, T (2003) *Beyond budgeting*. Harvard: Harvard Business School Press.

BARUCH LEV (2001) *Intangibles: management, measurement and reporting*. Washington: The Brookings Institution.

KAPLAN, R. and NORTON, D. (1996) *The balanced scorecard – translating strategy into action*. Harvard: Harvard Business School Press.

KEARNS, P. (2000) *Maximising your ROI in training*. London: Financial Times/Prentice-Hall.

KEARNS, P. (2000) *Measuring and managing employee performance*. London: Financial Times/Prentice Hall.

KEARNS, P. (2002) *The bottom line HR function*. London: Spiro Publishing.

KEARNS, P. (2003) *HR strategy: business focused, individually centred*. Oxford: Butterworth Heinemann.

KEARNS, P. (2004) *From trainer to learning consultant: an evolution*. Cambridgeshire: Training Journal (a series of 12 articles).

KEARNS, P. (2004) *Human capital management – One stop guide.* Sutton: Reed Business Information

KIRKPATRICK, D.L. (1998) *Evaluating training programs: the four levels.* (2nd ed) San Francisco: Berrett-Koehler. p 23.

LUNDIN, S.C., PAUL, H. and CHRISTENSEN, J. (2000) *Fish! A remarkable way to boost morale and improve results.* New York: Hyperion.

MINTZBERG, H. (2003) *Managers not MBAs.* London: FT Prentice Hall.

OHMAE, K. (1991) *The mind of the strategist.* Maidenhead: McGraw-Hill.

PFAU, B. (2001) *The human capital edge.* Maidenhead: McGraw Hill (Pfau also works for Watson Wyatt and their Human Capital Index).

PHILLIPS, J.J. (1983) *Handbook of training evaluation and measurement methods.* Houston, Texas: Gulf Publishing.

PHILLIPS, J.J. (1991) *Handbook of training evaluation and measurement methods.* (2nd ed) Houston, Texas: Gulf Publishing.

PHILLIPS, J.J. (1996) *Technical and skills training.* Alexandria, Virginia: American Society for Training and Development.

RUCCI A.J., KIM, S.P. and QUINN, R.T. The employee-customer profit chain at Sears *Harvard Business Review.* January – February 1998.

SCARBOROUGH, H, (2003) *The change agenda, human capital external reporting framework.* London: CIPD.

SENGE, P. (1993) *The fifth discipline: the art and practice of the learning organization.* London: Random House.

WARR, P., BIRD, M., and RACKCAM, N. (1978) *Evaluation of management training.* London: Gower.

■ INDEX

The Coach's Coach

Personal development for personal developers

Alison Hardingham
with Mike Brearley, Adrian Moorhouse and Brendan Venter

Being a coach is a tricky job, so whether you are an experienced coach or just starting out, a specialist consultant or a coaching manager, this book will help you become better and enjoy coaching more. It will help you to help the people you are coaching improve their performance – which, after all, is why you became a coach in the first place.

Alison Hardingham is a successful business coach and offers advice, techniques and examples drawn from experience of coaching people in all kinds of organisations and with the contributions of three phenomenally successful sports people: Mike Brearley, Adrian Moorhouse and Brendan Venter, you will be on track to being 'coach of the year'.

Mike Brearly is one of England's best known and most successful cricket captain; **Adrian Moorhouse** broke the world record in breast stroke five times and won an Olympic gold medal; and **Brendan Venter** was a member of the Springboks, South African Rugby Team, and subsequently played and coached at London Irish.

Order your copy now by visiting us online at www.cipd.co.uk/bookstore or call us on 0870 800 3366

Alison Hardingham is a business psychologist with more than twenty years' experience of coaching individuals and teams. She is a successful author and conference speaker.

| 2004 | 1 84398 075 4 | Paperback | 216 pages |

The Chartered Institute of Personnel and Development is the leading publisher of books and reports for personnel and training professionals, students, and for all those concerned with the effective management and development of people at work.

The New Rules of Engagement

How many of your employees care enough about their work, or your organisation, to do anything more than the bare minimum?

Highly engaged employees are six times less likely to be planning to leave their employer than the disengaged. Six times! How much could you save on your recruitment costs by improving engagement? How about the 'discretionary effort' that highly engaged employees put in?

Mike Johnson argues that there are ways to develop a new psychological contract between employer and employee. You can start by recognising that talk of 'work–life balance' is the wrong way round as far as your employees are concerned – they're much more interested in their 'life–work balance'. Their life always comes before your work. If you can find a way of accommodating that, then you're well on the way to getting their attention, engagement and commitment.

The advice in this book will:
- help you convince senior management that employee engagement matters
- help you to improve your employees' productivity and willingness to try out new ideas and work practices
- help you to retain key employees
- make it easier for you to attract a better calibre of new employee

This book offers practical, down-to-earth solutions that human resource and general managers can use to re-energise their employees (and themselves!).

'MBA professors should not put this book on their students' reading lists. It may change their attitude towards the rest of the syllabus. Mike Johnson tells it like it is. This book is a wake up call for real people managers from the "get real" school of management.'
Anne Chivers Head of Learning & Organisation Development, Housing Corporation

For a free sample chapter visit www.cipd.co.uk/bookstore

| 2004 | 1 84398 072 X | Paperback | 192 pages |

The Chartered Institute of Personnel and Development is the leading publisher of books and reports for personnel and training professionals, students, and for all those concerned with the effective management and development of people at work.

CIPD Policies and Procedures for People Managers

Sign Up for Your FREE 28-Day Trial Now and Save!

As a subscriber to *CIPD Employment Law for People Managers* you are entitled to an extra **10%** discount off the usual price of **CIPD Policies and Procedures for People Managers.**

Do you have time to create good practice policies compliant with the law?

Do you know what policies you ought to have in place?

Do you need resources to manage the HR function in your organisation?

Well, now help is at hand!

At the CIPD we are ideally placed to offer you example policies and procedures along with expert commentary.

In *Policies and Procedures for People Managers* you will find policies, procedures and documents covering every aspect of employment from recruitment to termination. Policies and procedures for every work scenario.

As part of your subscription all these documents are also *available free online* for you to download and adapt to your organisation's requirements.

What will I receive?

CIPD Policies and Procedures for People Managers is built around a loose-leaf volume including:

The manual – a comprehensive resource contained within an A4 binder

Updates – issued four times a year, these comprise the latest developments and legislative changes to keep the manual completely up to date, making sure you avoid problems in the future by ensuring that your policies and procedures are current now

Internet access – providing searchable unlimited access to the full service, including downloadable policies and procedures for you to adapt

Free book – a best-selling title from CIPD Publishing's portfolio, giving you further vital information.

To find out more, visit www.cipd.co.uk/ppfpm

CIPD Members	Non-members
~~Usual price £270~~	~~Usual price £300~~
You pay £245	You pay £270

Call 0870 442 1020 quoting media code EL1004 to get these special rates

Remember, you pay nothing for 28 days. If you are not entirely satisfied with *CIPD Policies and Procedures for People Managers*, you can return it with no further obligation.

Request your free 28-day trial of *CIPD Policies and Procedures for People Managers* today! Call 0870 442 1020 quoting media code EL1004

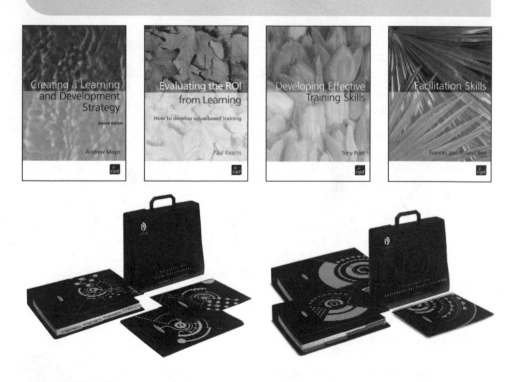